Out of the Whirlwind

*The Lord answered Job out of the whirlwind*
Job 38.1

Rex Chapman

# Out of the Whirlwind

SCM PRESS LTD

*To Gordon who set me thinking*
*To Tom and Basil who gave me the*
*freedom to think and*
*To the students who forced these*
*particular thoughts out of me*

334 01196 5

First published 1971
by SCM Press Ltd
56 Bloomsbury Street London WC1

© SCM Press Ltd 1971

Printed in Great Britain by
Northumberland Press Ltd
Gateshead

# Contents

Introduction                                    vi

The Early Days                                   1

The Tablets of Stone                            17

Joshua and the Judges                           29

Four Kings, Four Prophets                       37

Prophetic Writings                              57

Wisdom                                          97

The Unveiling of the Future                    107

Appendix 1: A Brief Bibliography               113

Appendix 2: Some Dates and Facts               114

Index of Passages                              117

# Introduction

I hope that we are now over the hump. I hope that we are nearing the time when we can read the Bible as literature and not feel that we have to emasculate its vitality by labelling it 'holy' – set apart into the lonely limbo-land of unread bestsellers. It is true of course that the language, thought-patterns and ideas of the Old Testament (with which this book is concerned) present many difficulties. It is even more true that some of the stories within it seem (and sometimes are) almost totally unedifying to the contemporary Christian trying his best to see what relevance they have to his everyday life as he sits in his pew and listens to such incidents as that of Jael driving a tent-peg through the head of Sisera. Yet in spite of this the Old Testament is important for any understanding of the New.

My first suggestion to the user of the meditations in this book is that he tries to forget that he is focussing his attention on 'Holy Scripture'. Let him rather read the Old Testament as literature in one of the modern translations available. Let him not be inhibited by the thought that he somehow *ought* to be making sense of what is there. Let him allow the Old Testament to stand on its own feet. If it illuminates his experience, well and good. If it does not, then not to worry. The Bible stands or falls by what it has to say.

My second suggestion to the general reader, therefore, is that he makes use of a modern commentary on the Old Testament to discover as far as possible just what the writings are saying. The meditations which follow presuppose not only that the passages on which they are based will be read, but also that some attempt will be made to consider their historical and cultural context. It is only then that we are in a position to reflect on and to pray the Bible. Here it is possible to give only very brief notes to introduce each section of the prayers. Mark Gibbard ssjE in his book *Why Pray?* (see appendix) writes that 'if anyone means to use the Bible effectively in his exploration of living and praying, he must know the main stream of the events which the Bible records and interprets. No one can really understand the significance of particular biblical passages unless he sees them in their original setting in the history of the Jewish people.' The reader is encouraged therefore to read, reflect and pray.

My third suggestion to the reader concerns the debate on the 'objectivity' of prayer. Is God myth or for real? Is there Someone, some Person, Something outside and beyond (or within and underneath) the world of matter and the world of experience? Or is the 'Lord' addressed in these meditations a projection in my mind, a figment of my imagination conjured up solely for the purposes of answering deep emotional needs? Is it rather like the common experience we might feel after being involved in a discussion? We go away to find ideas flooding our minds and kick ourselves for not having thought of them at the time; and perhaps we articulate them for ourselves and think them through *as if* we were still engaged in dialogue. It is in these sort of terms that the contemporary discussion continues. And here we are at an impasse. It is a discussion which cannot resolve in any objective sense. At the end of the day we have to live with the problem.

I suspect that our own understanding of prayer (whatever that might be) either authenticates itself in our own experience, at least to a sufficient degree for us to continue with it even through the most arid periods, or it has been long since given up, or perhaps not started at all. Our own experience, the value we attach to it and how we interpret it is in the last analysis the deciding factor for us. Reasons probably come later. In this respect it is the same with prayer as with all the intangible personal and aesthetic experiences by which we feel encountered. For I do believe that at the heart of prayer is an experience of 'encounter' which alone can make sense of and put meaning into the symbols and language of 'God-talk'.

This is not to say of course that those who find themselves unable to give any meaning to such a concept as 'encounter' do not pray; there are many no doubt whose lives are enriched and whose social consciences are made acute by 'reflecting in depth' on themselves and on the world around them, but whose reflections do not include any address to a 'Thou' or a 'Lord' or a 'God'. But it is to say that the only basis that I can see for the use of language about *God*, at least within the Christian tradition, is some experience, however transitory, however fragmentary, however fitful – and it is no more than this for most of us most of the time – that can be called an experience of or an encounter with the 'Other', with God. I see no possibility, however, of ever getting behind the experience to some 'reality' that is somehow distinct from the experience. We are left to our own interpretation of the experience. And we are back again to the impasse, the fundamental ambiguity of our experiences. Is God, or isn't he? Part of me wants to affirm the reality of the encounter, to shout 'yes' loud and clear, but part of me wonders and questions and doubts.

My suggestion to the reader is that he allows himself a period of peace and quiet in which simply to be silent or to reflect and think as he himself feels best in the light of his understanding of how other Christians have prayed and do pray. How he does this, how often he does it and how much time he gives to it are his own affair. The purpose is to become open to encounter the 'dimension of God' within human experience.

I offer the meditations in this book as a small contribution to the wholeness of prayer and as an example of a way into prayer which I personally find meaningful. They are meant to be complementary to my previous book, *A Kind of Praying*, as an attempt to bring together one man's contemporary experience and that of the community which produced and used, in this case, the Old Testament in the hope that something creative may be the result. Any understanding of spirituality is helped as much by considering how people do in fact pray as by a theoretical discussion of the subject.

The meditations which follow cover many of the more well-known stories and myths, historical narratives and theological interpretation, prophetic insight and practical teaching that comprise much of the Old Testament. Some of them have appeared in the weekly bulletin of the Anglican Chaplaincy to the University and Colleges in Aberdeen and I acknowledge my gratitude for the comments they have occasioned there from students and staff. I also express my indebtedness to the many people whose ideas have so informed my own that I am no longer aware of them as distinct from my own. Finally, I wish to thank my wife for a number of suggestions in the preparation of these reflections and for a great deal of encouragement.

REX CHAPMAN

viii

# The Early Days

In the opening section of these meditations we focus our attention on some of the biblical stories and narratives from Adam to Moses. For the general reader unacquainted with the light modern scholarship throws on the creation and other myths in the early chapters of the book of Genesis and on these accounts of the early history of Israel within the second millennium BC, we suggest the use of one of the commentaries mentioned in the appendix. These legends and narratives in their own context are speaking about man, his actions, his beliefs and his values, and therefore raise in our own minds questions as to the meaning of life which require from us some kind of answer.

# Adam is Everyman

Genesis 1.26-3.24

It was all her fault, said Adam.
It was all the snake's fault, said Eve.
It was all God's fault, say I.
This is where the buck stops.
You cannot get out of your responsibilities, Lord, any more than
    we can.
And thank God that you cannot.
'And God saw everything that he had made, and behold, it was very
    good.'
And yet we have the sin of Adam, the sin of man.
Why build it this way, Lord?
What on earth are you up to?
It seems odd.
If I did not know your presence,
If I did not have some small experience of your life,
If I did not have some assurance that you were on the side of man,
I would never believe.
But I do, and the problem remains.
I am aware of my pride, of my desire to become like a god.
But you are the 'ground of my being', the source of my life.
Between us, Lord,
In spite of an unfortunate beginning,
For heaven's sake let us make a go of it.
Let us not 'leave it to the snake'.
Stop me setting myself up in competition.
Draw me, and everyman, into your creative process in life.

# Cain is a Marked Man

Genesis 4.1-16

The 'tiller of the ground' killed the 'keeper of sheep'.
Fresh from Eden we are at each other's throats.
The soldiers of the Arabs fight the soldiers of the Jews.
The men from the management stand over against the men from the
    union.
There are two sides to every issue.
We fit into our roles in life and look out at the world from within
    them.
We are within with our friends.
Others are without.
This man is a teacher, that one a priest.
He is a bus driver, she is an accountant.
He is a labourer, she is a student.
There is no surprise, Lord, when jealousy and anxiety and anger
    rise between us, if all we see are people characterized by their
    functions.
Give us wisdom to see the other man's view of life.
Give us courage to divest ourselves of our formal roles.
You put your mark on Cain.
You protect him still.
Our divisions matter to you, Lord.
Mark us out for reconciliation.

# The Chaotic Flood

Genesis 6.5-8.19

Was there a vindictive side to these people, Lord – the people who
   wrote of the Flood?
Perhaps so, to have pictured you in the way they did, like the
   artist losing his temper with his work because he could not get
   it right.

The forces of chaos shatter all order.
They seek to drown a man's hopes, his plans, his career.
They well up inside and out to destroy all in their path.
They despoil the very necessities of life.
They leave behind them a train of refugees fleeing from war.
They bring a man's life to a halt in a crisis of indecision.
It is as if you were displeased with your creation, Lord, and were
   bringing it to nought.
And yet for the man who is ready these same forces sweep him on
   his way to the re-creation of life.
Chaos contains within it the slight glimmer of hope.
Lord, you are there.
You are in life.
You are in the Flood.
You are in the midst.
Send me, send everyman, the dove with the olive leaf in its mouth.

# Sons of Noah

Genesis 9.18-19

The whole earth, they write, was peopled from the sons of Noah.
It all begins with *our* race.
Galaxies circle the earth, they say. Galileo is wrong!
We are the summit of creation, untarred by evolution.

We like to be at the centre, Lord, in these matters as in all things.
But knowledge brings humility in its train.
Give us knowledge.

# Babel

Genesis 11.1-9

It was Babel, Lord.
Feelings ran high.
Hostilities were expressed.
Aggression came to the surface.
Anxiety was acute.
Embarrassment was intense.
The hidden agenda was hidden no more.
Many were shocked to find our seeming fellowship as brittle as bone
    china.
We were afraid of the feelings.
We withdrew into ourselves at first, and spoke only to launch an
    attack or to make a disguised cry for help.
This conference was your church, Lord, and we were in chaos.
There we were for two days to discuss responsibility.
There we were seeking to be the church.
Yet we might as well have been scattered over the face of all the
    earth.
Were you there, Lord, as we faced each other?
Were you there as we glimpsed the inner emotions that burst from
    the depth of our souls?
Were you there as we strove to pick up the pieces and bind ourselves
    together?
Lord, be there – especially there.

# Abraham's Faith and Mine

Genesis 12.1-4, 22.1-14

It is an incredible story, Lord, with its trace of child sacrifice.
What was he like – the real man behind the story, the flesh and
blood man who epitomizes faith?
And the Lord said: Go from your country and your kindred; ...
so Abraham went.
And the Lord said: Take your son; ... so he arose early in the
morning and took his son Isaac.

Faith is knowing, yet not knowing,
Being sure, yet unsure,
Having certainty, yet being uncertain.
Faith is a man's conviction of what he must do,
$\qquad\qquad\qquad$ who he will be,
$\qquad\qquad\qquad$ how he will live,
And always the end is shrouded in mist.

Lord, I believe.
I have faith.
I stake all on the ultimacy of hope.
The alternative is darker than my 'cloud of unknowing'.
Come, Lord, and let me call this place 'The Lord will provide'.

# Dreams

Genesis 28.10-22 (27.1-29)


There were no railings, no people, no protection, nothing.
Water was sweeping past, faster and faster, falling away at her
feet.
She was standing above the waterfall, terrified, feeling her feet
giving way beneath her as the water tempted her to follow into
the abyss ...
And then she awoke.

We have no conscious control in our sleep.
The inner springs of personality, the sense of well-being or of fear,
surface for the night.
Do dreams perhaps reveal our hidden feelings, our state of mind?
Truly, Lord, you were in the mind of a man guilty over the decep-
tion of his father.
Truly you are somewhere in the mind of the woman waking in a
sweat.
Truly you are in this place even when I do not know it.

# It is a Struggle to Pray

Genesis 32.24-30

It is a struggle to pray, Lord.
It takes time and energy.
It conflicts so much with a modern view of things.
It is far easier to find an excuse.
   I am too busy.
   I am come of age.
   I must look for God in my daily involvement in the world.
And I know that I must, Lord, but I need time too to reflect and
   think and pray – a 'space' to recollect your presence in my in-
   volvement in your world.

But it is a struggle to pray,
To encounter you on the way, directing Jacob, directing me, turn-
   ing us round in our tracks to follow quite a different route.
And it is a struggle that I think perhaps I might even win.
You give me the freedom to choose, to decide, to go my own way.
But you have got under my skin.
And there you undermine my pride, my will to stand on my own,
And yet you strengthen my morale, invigorating me with your
   power.
You struggle with me and alongside me, and make me part of your
   plan.
Lord, I have seen you face to face, and my life is preserved.

# How Joseph Travelled from Canaan to Egypt

Genesis 37.5-28

Fancy telling them of such a dream!
Was he so naive, Lord?
Was it part of a campaign by the youngest of the family to claim
some status?
You may all be older and more powerful and assured, but I dream
dreams that reveal our future roles reversed.

It is a universal problem, Lord.
The younger, less experienced man with ties that hold him linked
together with another, is the ready target for hostilities if he
'rises above his station'.
And more. He becomes like the man marked out for leadership who
bears the brunt of the emotions of the led.
He becomes like the man whose talents are discounted by those
who are disturbed by them and retaliate by pointing to their own.
What hope of reconciliation with barriers such as these?

Give me, give all men, Lord, a sense of our worth.
Give us the will to develop to the full whatever you have placed
within us.
Give us the assurance to become what we are in your scheme of
things.
Then, perhaps, our relationships will become less fraught with
anxiety and jealousy.
Then, perhaps, a man's journey from Canaan to Egypt might be
surrounded with less anger.

# Fourteen Cows, Seven Fat, Seven Thin

Genesis 39.21, 41.1-45, 45.4-5


Crafty old Joseph!

From rags to riches via an astute interpretation of the fourteen cows.

He had mastered the art of 'how to win friends and influence people',

He had survived the ill will of his brothers.

He had ridden the anger of a jilted woman.

He was to hold down his new job through the dangers of high office.

He was no better than the next man, Lord, but you were with him 'and showed him steadfast love'.

It helped him to forgive his brothers when he was in a position to take revenge.

Joseph is more than the hero of this romantic story, Lord.

He exists in every generation, in every place, wherever men are.

He is a man who is full of human failings, but who has some awareness too of being caught up in your purposes and your will for the world.

'For God sent me to preserve life.'


Take me, Lord.

Overcome my weaknesses.

Send me into your world to preserve life and to give life.

# The Day Moses Saw the Bush

Exodus 3, 4.10-16

A burning bush became a focus, Lord, for a man's mind to grapple
  with the problems of his future.
Did the task seem too great?
Did he wonder why it should be he who had to give a lead to his
  people?
Did he resent having to leave the security of his married life in
  Midian, looking after sheep?
Yet he could not rest content.
The voice within him became more insistent.
No longer could he put off a decision and push the internal ques-
  tioning to the back of his mind.
The day he saw the bush, he knew what he must do, apprehensive
  though he was.
Be with those, Lord, who have decisions to make about themselves,
  about others.
Be with me as I face up to the decisions I have to make.
Let me, let us, not miss the signs.

# A Rough Sea Crossing

Exodus 14.5-31

Valuable slave labour was being lost.
So the Pharaoh, like the Grand Old Duke of York, marched after
    them with all his horses and all his men.
But the odds were stacked against him.
And when they were down they were down.

The people of Israel glimpsed something of your power, Lord.
They looked back on the events hidden beneath this tale of the sea
    crossing as a sure sign of your favour.
But they saw you as a one-sided God, and that side was theirs.

Your church, Lord, is sometimes tempted to take this view,
You are made to stand with the church over against the world.
The one will drown while the other goes marching on.
Widen our vision, Lord.
You have ultimate charge of your world.
You can master forces as wild as the sea.
You are the God of Pharaoh, and of Moses, and of me.
Bring my understanding of your power to maturity.

# An Ark for Salvation?

Exodus 25.10-22

It is too easy to pin you down, Lord.
It makes life much easier.
It gives us that bit more control over your unpredictability.
You are met here, or there, but not anywhere else.
You are in the ark, or the sanctuary, or the church building.
We can come there if we want to get in touch.
Don't call me; I will call you.
We can prepare ourselves for the meeting, for the encounter, once
    we know where you are to be found.
We can get into the frame of mind for worship, adoration, prayer.
'You don't expect to find a spare room with us, do you?
We built you a house to call your own.
What more can a reasonable God expect?'[1]
Don't worry, God; we will give you a space.
We can even cart you off into battle as a mascot, and give you a
    tent of your own.
Break through this parody, Lord.
Break into my life now, in my concerns and worries,
                my joys and delights,
                my activities and engagements,
    in the places I visit and the people I meet.
Let those things, those buildings, those places that focus our
    attention on you do simply this.
You are to be encountered there, because you are to be encountered
    everywhere.

[1] Chad Walsh, from *The Destruction by Fire of the Beloit Chapel*.

# Aaron's Uncertainty

Exodus 32.1-6

It was the uncertainty of it all.
He had been gone so long.
He might have been killed on the mountain.
'Come, make us a god to go at the head of us.'

It was the uncertainty of it all.
He had gone, dead and buried these three days.
He had been killed.
'Come, make us a god to go at the head of us.'

It is the uncertainty of it all.
Our knowledge, Lord, is the knowledge of faith, not of fact.
It is a knowledge with built-in question marks.
It is a knowledge that does not provide all the answers.
It is a knowledge that encourages us in 'living with questions'.
And there are lots of questions.
He has been gone so long.
Soon two thousand years will have passed.
Come, Lord, strengthen my faith.

# The Tablets of Stone

The Ten Commandments have traditionally occupied a place of importance within the church even though they antedate the life of Jesus by several centuries and are often said to have been superseded by Jesus' 'Summary of the Law'. It is true that their negative flavour makes them impracticable as a positive guide to living, but they do raise profound questions about life and this justifies our taking a closer look at them.

# Divinity All Round

Exodus 20.1-3

*You shall have no other gods before me.*
Fertility cults ran you close, Lord.
Fruitfulness in soil and people mattered to them greatly.
The turning of individuals into gods runs you close, Lord.
It seems often to matter greatly to that person over there who hangs
    from the words of another.
He looks up to him.
He accepts all that he says.
He sees him as a man who can do no wrong.
It seems often to matter greatly to myself that I set myself at the
    centre of my world.
I put myself at the hub of my universe.
There is divinity all round.
Enable me to base all that I am on you, Lord.
Not on myself.
Not on anyone else,
But on you.
Enable me to understand and feel and absorb humility.

# Idols Modern Style

Exodus 20.4-6

*You shall not make for yourself a graven image.*
It was almost impossible to sit down without the fear that this
  very act would make the room untidy.
The duster was much in evidence.
As were her irrational apologies for the untidiness of the place.
She tended her home as carefully as her husband polished his car.
Dust and dirt were banished as religiously as if they were sin.
We no longer make golden bulls, Lord, though some still fear the
  stars.
We turn our wealth into idols.
We invest things with a significance beyond their worth.
We have great expectations of fulfilment, of peace, of salvation,
  from activities, from things, from achievements.
Yet these never totally satisfy our hopes.
Lord, let me not despise this measure of fulfilment, partial though
  it be.
But let me cast my eyes beyond it to you who are the source of all.

# A Name in Vain

Exodus 20.7

*You shall not take the name of the Lord your God in vain.*
I spoke about (John), Lord.
I said more than I ought.
I generalized from massive ignorance.
I made sweeping statements based on so little knowledge.
God, what arrogance!
I took his name in vain.
I built up his personality into the shape I wanted.
I set myself up as the potter with his clay.
I made him someone he might not have been.
Enable me to take his humanity seriously, Lord.
Enable me too to take your divinity seriously.
You are who you are.
You will be who you will be.
Do I turn you into a totem by trying to define who you are?
Do I take your name in vain by uttering pious platitudes, then living
    as I wish?
Enable me to take seriously both you and my neighbour.

# The Problem of Sabbath

Exodus 20.8-11

*Remember the sabbath day to keep it holy.*
None of your continental Sundays, thank you!
No drink on the sabbath!
Six days you shall labour.
Remember the sabbath to keep it holy.
Isn't the sabbath Saturday, not Sunday?
I wish the problems were as superficial as this, Lord.
The problem is how to relax,
How to rest,
How to sit and do nothing.
How to loose the chains that bind me to activity,
How to let my mind empty of ideas and thoughts and tensions,
How to free myself from the whirlpool of feelings within.
The problem is how to use a time for tranquillity before that time
     has passed.
Bless my sabbath whenever it comes, Lord.
Hallow it.
Make it yours.
Fill it with your peace.

# Parents

Exodus 20.12

*Honour your father and your mother.*
Some attitudes to parents come to mind, Lord.
That teenage girl who feels 'misunderstood'.
That adolescent, restless and impatient as he grows in independence.
That elderly woman whose care is constant for her more elderly
    mother.
That child voracious and demanding.
That young woman, cultured and wise, who secretly feels embar-
    rassed to be seen with her mother.
That junior executive who half feels his father a fool.
That young man who resents his parents' concern for his welfare.
That girl and that man, away from home, who return from time
    to time to share in the welcome and to strengthen their sense
    of security and well-being.
That middle-aged woman, still at home and alone with her mother,
    dependent, afraid to meet people on her own, liable for collapse
    when mother dies.

It is impossible totally to ignore parents, Lord.
Much of what they have been and are is built into the soul.
It affects how a man thinks and feels and reacts – for good or bad.
It stays a part of his personality – perhaps until the day he dies.
It is there, sometimes seen, sometimes unseen, in his life and his
    relationships.
The past is carried within to influence the present.
Let a man come to terms with his parental past.
Let him be aware of the magnetic pull of those forces that formed
    his early surroundings.
Give him insight. Give him maturity.
This is honour to his parents.

# Killing

Exodus 20.13

Take a package tour of history, Lord.
Take a look at the bloody wars of the Bible.
You shall not kill?
They seemed to think that you were on their side.
Take a look at the aggression of that most civilized of peoples, the
    Athenians of Classical Greece.
The clinical and coldly devastating military machine of the Romans.
The barbaric wars of the Dark Ages.
The so-called religious wars of Christendom.
The madmen's wars of Napoleon and Hitler.
The mini-wars of major powers in Korea and Vietnam.
The individual slaughter of men hanging from a noose.
Killing makes a man less of a man.
At worst it dehumanizes him.
At best it assails him with guilt.
Can we really differentiate killing from murder?

And yet are there times when to end life is the lesser of evils?
Can a man look on while the strong annihilates the weak?
Can he look on while a pregnant woman cries for abortion?
Has he to step in and act?
I know what I feel.
I am not sure that it is right.
I am suspicious of men with the clear-cut answer.
Speak, Lord, whenever the situation comes, when a decision has to
    be made.
Help us to wrestle with the problems.

# Man and Woman

Exodus 20.14

Yet another negative command.
*You shall not commit adultery.*

That man's wife is attractive company and good to be with.
She is wise and sane, married with young children.
He is talented and friendly, unmarried and on his own.
He occasionally calls for a chat, and talks and talks and talks about
　his job, his ideas, his hopes.
Their friendship strengthens them both.
Is the only guide to our relationships in these blocks of stone to
　be this negative one, Lord?
Adultery is not always one of the options.
The man who makes commandments seeks no doubt for social
　stability.
He worries about consequences.
Is he so afraid of feelings, of emotions, that he is compelled to
　forbid?
Why not some word about love, about friendship, about the healthy
　and good meeting of man and woman?
Lord, you give the word:
'You shall love your neighbour as yourself.'
In Jesus you enjoyed the company of women.
Strengthen our relationships with your love.

# Property is Sacred, They Say

Exodus 20.15; Acts 2.42-45

*You shall not steal.*
Property is sacred.
Things are possessions.
Goods are mine, or yours, or his.
'All whose faith had drawn them together held everything in common.'
But of course it did not work, they say.
People do not look after that which isn't their own, they say.
Society cannot be run on these lines, they say.
Property is sacred.
You shall not steal.

My indignation is a little forced, Lord.
I feel, yes I feel, idealistic, and hear a voice within me crying in the wilderness of possessions.
But there is much of me too that senses that what they say contains some truth.
Some of the things a man has and treasures and takes a delight in are an expression of himself, an extension of who he is.
To remove these things without asking is to make a man unsure of his surroundings.
It is to make the basis of life the uncertainty of distrust.

Loosen our hold, Lord, on things.
Let us not wallow in grasping tightly to what rightly needs to be shared.
Free us to be responsible guardians and givers of what we have.

# Witness the Truth

Exodus 20.16

*You shall not bear false witness.*
There are the reasonably clear-cut deceptions, Lord.
The small boy blaming it all on to his friend.
The young woman telling of the mythical advances of a neighbouring priest.
The down and out man asking yet again for the price of a cup of tea, his euphemism for anything alcoholic.
Some more serious than others.
Sometimes a person cannot stand the truth and has to lie.

Sometimes he is pushed to the limits of his endurance and gives false witness to his real feelings.
There was the woman who was very tired.
She had been working non-stop for weeks.
She was under considerable pressure,
On edge : her nerves as taut as a bow string.
And finally they snapped.
Her bottled-up feelings were unleashed against the man she loved.

Sometimes false witness takes an insidious form.
No deception is meant.
But a man speaks and judges and draws conclusions about another and thinks that he tells the truth.
What he reveals are his prejudices and biases mixed perhaps with a little truth.

Lord, you are truth.
Dwell within me so that I see others as they are.
Dwell within me so that I have no need to distort the truth.

# The Ox and the Ass

Exodus 20.17

*You shall not covet.*
None of my neighbours employs either a manservant or a
    maidservant whom I could covet, Lord.
And I don't particularly want an ox or an ass.
Nor indeed have I got my eye on anyone's wife.
I could list many things that I have no desire to possess.
Covetousness, envy, desire are very personal things, Lord.
They attach themselves to a man as closely as a leech.
They attack at our weakest spots and leave us in no doubt of their
    presence.
But they differ for different people.
One man has a passion to reach that 'room at the top'.
Another lusts for a bigger and better model of something he already
    has.
Another covets the reassurance without which he feels incomplete.
Yet another envies a friend's success; he cannot stand someone so
    close enjoying a success of which he himself feels deprived.

Reveal clearly, Lord, the ox and the ass, the things a man covets.
Reveal clearly the things I covet.
Separate them from those aims and objects that I should rightly
    strive to achieve.
Set my mind on your Kingdom before everything else.

# Joshua and the Judges

The down to earth, yet profound, story of Ruth (set in the period of the Judges though written at a much later date) contrasts with the aggressive conquest of Canaan by the Yahweh-inspired armies of Joshua and the Judges. The actual events of the settlement at the end of the second millennium BC lie buried beneath this theological interpretation and for further information concerning this we would refer the reader to a modern commentary. Here we are concerned to let the stories feed our imagination and lead us to reflect and pray.

In the first two passages of this section we consider the story of Rahab and the fall of Jericho. Rahab, the prostitute, gives sanctuary to two of Joshua's agents as they spy out the city of Jericho with a view to its conquest. The scarlet cord she hangs from her house affords her protection when the invading army totally destroys the city.

From the stories of the Judges we have selected those of Gideon and Samson. Gideon is said to defeat the Midianites with a small section of his army, though he refuses to accept the title of king. The Samson saga concerns an unsophisticated hero, consecrated in infancy to Yahweh, who reveals the secret of his power to Delilah and is thereupon taken captive by the Philistines. The saga ends with a final appeal to Yahweh, which results in the simultaneous death of Samson and of many of his enemies. Samson symbolizes the consecrated yet wayward nature not only of Israel but of mankind as a whole.

The story of Ruth, the Moabitess remaining loyal to Naomi after the death of her own husband and eventually marrying Boaz, ends this section of meditations with a peaceful challenge to the exclusivism of Israel.

# The Harlot's Scarlet Cord

Joshua 2.1-21

Perhaps she knew which side her bread was buttered, Lord.
It would not do to incur your wrath.
Perhaps she was playing safe to ensure the good will of both sides.
Or had she simply been well paid for her trouble?
Perhaps I am too cynical, Lord.
She may have been concerned for the welfare of two individuals.
Few actions are so pure that there is no room for doubt.
The silent voice within urged her to a risk.
However mixed the motives she is said to acknowledge your power.
Even though the decision has the mark of self-concern, that acknow-
    ledgment of your power is the scarlet cord marking her out too
    as yours.

I, like all, am concerned for my welfare.
It is at the front of my mind directing my life – a biological drive
    for self-preservation, a psychological need for security.
Open my eyes to see beyond the matter-of-fact existence that sur-
    rounds me.
Open my eyes to see to the heart of the matter.
Open my eyes to see how you would have me co-operate with your
    will.
Open my eyes to see that 'the Lord your God is he who is God in
    heaven above and on earth beneath'.

# And the Walls Came Tumbling Down

Joshua 6.1-27

Hiroshima, Dresden, Jericho.
Atom bomb, blanket bombing, total destruction.
And the walls came tumbling down.
The conquest of the land.
The waters of the Elbe and the Jordan share their common know-
    ledge.
A crushing blow to weaken morale and cut months off the war.
A city 'devoted to the Lord for destruction'.
And 'the Lord was with Joshua, and his fame was in all the land'.

Some fame!
Some Lord!
Rationalized retribution.
Power pushed to an extreme.
Full rein given to hate.
You are at work in the forces of history, Lord.
You guide, you direct, you support.
But am I to believe that you are the Destroyer?
Three thousand years have passed and we still want you on our
    side in our destroying.
Give us the wisdom to see through our passions, to work for that
    peace which is beyond understanding.

# Gideon's Gallant Three Hundred

Judges 7.1-25, 8.22-23


No danger of overkill with an army reduced to three hundred, until
    the reinforcements were called in.
A surprise attack in the dead of night and victory was theirs.
He attributes his success to you, Lord, and refuses kingship.
There is something striking about this.
It is more usual to claim success for oneself, and to save for you or
    for others the blame when things go wrong.
I like the credit, but not the blame.
I like it when things go well, rejoicing in responsibility.

Gideon said: 'I will not rule over you, and my son will not rule
    over you; the Lord will rule over you.'
Yours is the ultimate power, Lord.
You work through a man's life and his actions.
Work through mine.
Enable me both to take responsibility and yet have the humility to
    let whatever may be good within me point beyond myself to you.

# Samson

Judges 13.2-16.31

The nation in a man.
Consecrated, but broken,
Ending 'eyeless in Gaza'.

Mankind in a man.
Blessed by God, but wayward,
Finding himself 'at the mill with slaves'.

Crude and uncultured,
A man for riddles,
But your man, Lord.

Life is a riddle.
Your man, my own man.
Whose man in the end?

# Black, White, Brown, Yellow

Ruth

They burst into a bedroom, so it is said, to catch the copulation of
    White with Black.
Apartheid must be preserved.
There is a place for the White and a place for the Black, and that
    place is in separate beds.

Boaz bedded down with a Gentile to father the father of David.
Israel's ancestry is mixed.
The boundaries are blurred of the people of God.
What greater protest is there, Lord, at narrow exclusivism?
My race right or wrong!
The story might beguile even the man who says: 'I wouldn't want
    my daughter to marry one of them. Think of the children!'
Think of David, the eventual fruit of the marriage, the symbol of
    the Messiah.

Man is full of prejudice, Lord.
Reveal mine clearly to me.
Let me understand the facts.
Have me base my views on knowledge.
Unite men, Lord.
Unite us to one another.
Be the focus of our reconciliation.
'Where you go I will go and where you lodge I will lodge; and your
    people shall be my people, and your God my God.'

# Four Kings, Four Prophets

Saul, David, Solomon and Ahab are the kings, Samuel, Nathan, Elijah and Elisha the prophets. Some of the more well-known incidents associated with these eight characters (located historically within the period from the end of the eleventh century to the second half of the ninth) in the Books of Samuel and Kings are the 'starters' for the following meditations. Much of the historical material found within the Old Testament seems to the modern reader almost totally unedifying as well as being often crude and irrelevant. Yet the stories we have selected deal with intensely human individuals expressing their faith (and un-faith) in God within their own cultural milieu. The God of David and of Elijah is also the God and Father of Jesus Christ even though their understanding of God may have differed considerably. We doubt whether it is possible to understand the life, teaching and ministry of Jesus without some attempt to grapple with and reflect on the traditions which formed his background.

# Hannah's Hope

1 Samuel 1.1-2.11

Drunk and disorderly.
The crystals turning green.
Keep off the bottle ...
It's all a mistake.
The big misunderstanding.
And indeed it was.
She had drunk the cup of sorrow, not of wine.
She wanted a child to complete her womanhood.
She wanted a child more than anything else.
She wanted a child.
Samuel.

She fussed and spoiled the children of others.
She wished they were hers.
She was often blind to their faults in her longing.
She sought to be an authority on children, to show that, even
  childless, she knew a thing or two.
Didn't you hear her prayer, Lord?
Didn't she pray as hard as Hannah?
And yet she too 'exults in the Lord'.
She is greater than Hannah, Lord.
In you she trusts,
Knowing that there will be no child.

# The Listening Servant

1 Samuel 3

A night in the temple to discover your will.
An 'incubation-oracle' they call it.
An egg is hatched!
A young man becomes aware of your presence.
'Speak, Lord, for your servant hears.'

Quiet,
Waiting,
Listening,
Freeing myself to attend.
Silent,
Attentive,
Relaxed,
Recalling your presence.
'Speak, Lord, for your servant hears.'

# Who is King?

1 Samuel 8.4-22, 10.17-25; 1 Peter 2.9

Appoint for us a king.
We have had enough of being a peculiar people, a chosen race, a
    holy nation.
Make us like all the rest, indistinguishable from the mass.
Give us a king.
We will be satisfied with nothing less.

When the vision fades,
When faith weakens,
When the experience is less compelling,
When the evidence no longer seems so weighty,
The temptation is strong to opt out of that response to you, Lord,
    that seemed so vital once.
The temptation is strong to opt out of the 'royal priesthood, the
    dedicated nation, the people claimed by God for his own'.
The light outside often seems no darker than that within.
The cry is loud:
Make us like all the nations.
Give us a king.

Your kingdom comes, Lord, and your will is done both there and
    here, inside and out, within the church and without.
Be the King, Lord,
Both there and here.

# David's Goliath

1 Samuel 17

It is a bit embarrassing that they attribute such a bloody slaughter
    to you, Lord.
They exult in it.
You are their leader and lord of war.

What's that you say?
I worry too much that the feelings and ideas and beliefs of cen-
    turies past are less than they ought to be?
Perhaps this is so.
To future generations our own ideals may seem barbaric.
But there is more to this story, Lord, and would that that more
    were mine!
I envy David his faith.
I envy him his certainty, his sure belief that you were standing
    firmly behind his life.
I envy him the courage to face a situation where the odds were
    stacked against him.
You support a man.
You reverse his values.
You use whatever resources are present within him.
You turn weakness into strength.
Let me not misuse my resources.
Rather let me know the assurance of your presence.

# Saul's Vendetta

1 Samuel 18.28-20.1

There were times of feeling miserable,
Times when nothing went right,
When the world seemed against him,
When he looked out on a blackness that revealed no glimmer of
    light.
He found it too painful to locate the centre of his problem within
    himself.
So he focussed his rage against David.
Here was the fault!
Here was the source of his trouble!
A man popular with the people, too successful for comfort.
Let him but be removed and I will return to my former glory!
The up-and-coming-man is often seen as a threat to the man who
    has arrived.
He is a possible successor, a man waiting for the chair to be vacated.
He must be kept in control, said 'the evil spirit' that came upon
    Saul.
It is hard for anything to seem right to the man with a grudge.
All that he sees is seen as a challenge.
All that is done is done to make him feel small.
Nothing can happen without it being a form of spite.

Let me give thanks, Lord, for all that is good in others.
Let me not seek to destroy it in a fit of paranoia.

# The Witch of Endor

1 Samuel 28.3-19, 31.1-7


'The medium is the message',
And the message is bad news.
Saul was at the end of the road.
Deprived of faith,
Deserted, he felt, by his Lord,
Driven in despair to consult a woman with a reputation for raising
    the spirits of the dead,
Desiring above all the miracle to allay his fear,
He was clutching at straws.
What else could be done, with no word from the Lord?
Surely Samuel, the ghost of time past, would give him comfort and
    help.
But the medium gave the message,
And the message was bad news.
Deranged and depressed he killed himself in defeat.
His life, Lord, is the stuff of tragedy.
It would be no honour to him to seek for the happy ending.

# The Magnanimity of David

2 Samuel 1.17-27

David was man enough to see some nobility in Saul.
'How are the mighty fallen!'
'Ye daughters of Israel, weep over Saul.'
He had been pursued by Saul, hunted and a target for his spear.
He might easily have written him off and blackened his name.
Was he sure enough of himself and of his status before God to have
    no need for climbing to fame by belittling his predecessor?
There was no need to scramble for a crown over the corpse of the
    king.
He saw that Saul, even in madness, was your man, Lord.
Here lies greatness in David.
Here is maturity.
Here is the mark of another man touched by you.

Develop within me, Lord, the power to see as objectively as you do,
To see what is the case,
To see the nature of a man,
Through the veil of my emotions and suspicions and pride.
Make me sure enough of myself and of my status before you to
    have no need for grasping at glory by lowering its value.

# A City of Hope and Despair

2 Samuel 5.1-6.15


Jerusalem is taken, to become the capital of David's Kingdom and
    one of the crossroads of history.
The home of Temple, Mosque and Cross.
The focus of love and faith and God.
The crucible of hate and anger and despair.
Its chequered career runs like a via dolorosa through the centuries,
    and onward into the future.
You did well, Lord, to be crucified there.
Where better than in a city that knows the sin of man?

Lord, reconcile and unite,
And not just there,
But here too, in the areas of my responsibility,
Where tensions remain unresolved,
In the perpetual anxiety of not knowing whether the place of meet-
    ing will produce further explosion or the seeds of reconciliation.
At whatever place men meet,
Wherever we come together,
Be there, Lord, now.

# 'You Are the Man'

2 Samuel 12.1-15

You could have heard a pin drop.
'You are the man.'
The silence was deafening.
How would he react?
What would he do?
What would he say?
Fingers were crossed; breaths were held.
A man of power and influence, he had been enticed into admitting
his guilt.
'You are the man.'
Would he deal with the prophet as ruthlessly as he had dealt with
the Hittite?
Would he have him killed, and then turn his anger against those
who had seen his humiliation?
What would he do?

The courage of the man – to confront the king with his sin!
'You are the man,' he said.
The courage of the man – to confess his sin to one who was in his
power!
'I am the man,' he confessed.

Lord, give me courage.

# That Proverbial Wisdom of Solomon

1 Kings 3.3-28

The one would rather the child die than that another woman
   should enjoy her motherhood.
Good fortune is the yearning of all.
When hopes are dashed, it takes great strength to survey another's
   joy.
Let me but grasp the child, and who will be any the wiser?
Let me seize another's happiness as my own, or if that is impossible,
   at least I may make her share my suffering.

The other would rather another woman have her child than that
   he should die.
She sacrifices her hopes in the interests of something greater.
She prepares to endure the pain of watching another reap the joy
   that ought to be hers by rights.
Let her have the child;
Let anything happen but that he should be slain.

Solomon's proverbial wisdom was based, it seems, on not a little
   insight into human feelings and emotions.
His rough-and-ready treatment was rooted in some knowledge of
   human nature.
And justice was seen to be done.

Increase my insight, Lord.
Let your wisdom grow within me.
For you are the wisdom of God.

# The House that Solomon Built

1 Kings 5, 7.51-8.13

The 'levy of forced labour out of all Israel' was thirty thousand
   strong.
There were seventy thousand 'burden-bearers',
And the eighty thousand 'hewers of stone in the hill-country'.
I wonder, Lord, what they thought about the costly dressed stones.
I wonder what they thought about 'all the timber of cedar and
   cypress' that Solomon desired from Lebanon.
How many of them survived the building?
Were they invited, do you think, to the opening ceremony?
Did they understand the doctrine of vicarious building in the decla-
   ration of the king?
'I have built you an exalted house, a place for you to dwell in for
   ever.'
He was proud of the work, the apple of his eye, a home for the ark.
'The glory of the Lord filled the house of the Lord.'

This is a small matter, Lord.
Be there, if you wish.
But far more important,
Be where people work and labour and sweat,
Where life is determined by forces beyond our control,
Wherever men are,
Be at the heart of humanity.
You reach out to a man wherever he is long before he thinks to
   structure the encounter in stone.

# Wealth, Wealth, Glorious Wealth

1 Kings 10.1-13

She came,
She saw,
She was conquered.
The Sheba trade mission was a glorious success.
Who doesn't crave for a wisdom that brings wealth in its train?
Wisdom and wealth are a winning combination.
'When the Queen of Sheba had seen all the wisdom of Solomon, the
    house that he had built, the food of his table ... the attendance
    of his servants, their clothing, their cupbearers, and his burnt
    offerings ... there was no more spirit within her.'

Who can resist the luxury that money can buy?
There would be no need to resist, Lord, if the luxury were shared
    by all.
Let Solomon enjoy his things, but only when all men are as wealthy
    as he.
Give us the wisdom that fosters wealth where it is needed most.

# More Miracles

1 Kings 17

More miracles.
More problems for modern man.
More explaining away to be done.
They are a source of difficulty rather than help.
I am fed up with miracles, Lord.
That food, like manna from heaven.
That raising of the dead.
If you worked in that way then, what on earth are you doing now?
Is it our lack of faith, or their credulity?
Elijah, the political prophet risking his life every time he intervened in the sordid affairs of Ahab and his wife, is emasculated by these popular folk tales.
It is untrue to my experience, Lord, to have you wading in with the magic touch.
You give men vision.
You support us as we seek to do your will.
You strengthen us as we falter beneath the forces that loom over us.
But you have given us freedom,
Freedom from capricious gods who sometimes do this and sometimes do not,
Freedom to be ourselves.
If men of greatness must be credited with legends,
Let Elijah have his.
But let us not pretend that the heart of the matter is here.
Let us not hide from the realities of living and dying as men with our own decisions to make.

# Contest on Carmel

1 Kings 18.17-40

It's too good to be true!
A bonfire laid on at the decisive moment,
So that they say 'The Lord, he is God; the Lord, he is God.'
Let the prophets of Baal be killed!
I wonder, Lord, what event lies hidden beneath this scene.
Was there some natural occurrence that Elijah could use as a sign
from heaven?
The prophets of Baal are always more numerous than those of
yours.
Their lot is so much easier.
It makes me as desirous as Elijah of some display of power, to re-
assure a flagging spirit.
And yet I can't believe that you were vying with the thunderbolts
of Zeus.
You are the Lord,
You are God.
You are not some deity who has to prove his power with a show of
strength.
Your presence is more subtle, more profound.
You are within the life of a man enticing him to faith.
No 'big bang' proof can take the place of the continuous creating
and deepening of a man's awareness of you and of others.
Your show of power is the weakness and folly of the Cross.
Your show of power is your death.
And in this is life for me.

# What is Hidden in the Earthquake?

1 Kings 19.1-18

I feel surrounded by earthquakes, Lord,
Cataclysmic events within the experience of those around me,
Powerful pressures working as 'hidden persuaders' to effect their
    demands upon me.
It's when the heat is on that I covet the reassuring touch of Elijah's
    angel.
It's when the heat is on that I feel most on my own, wearing the
    shoes in which no one else can stand.
'But the Lord was not in the earthquake.'

I cannot believe, Lord, that you only turn up when the action is
    over,
When a man withdraws into the silence of the 'still small voice'.
You were there at the Cross,
In the shouting, mocking crowd,
In the tumult of Golgotha,
You were there as a man.
Is this perhaps the point?
Does 'your presence take the form of absence, giving a vote of
    confidence in man'?
When the chips are down is your presence totally hidden to the
    man on the spot?
'My God, my God, why have you forsaken me?'
You lead a man to maturity when his back is to the wall.
Is his presence in the earthquake your hidden presence, Lord?

# The Vineyard that Caused the Sulk

1 Kings 21

We would expect it of a child.
We expect a child to sulk if he does not get his own way.
But Ahab was the king.
It was only a small vineyard, but he wanted it more than anything
   else.
And he was offering a good price.
His desire was kindled the more by Naboth's refusal to sell.
So he went off his food and sulked.
But his wife wore the trousers and contrived to give him his wish
   to cheer him up.
Even kings, it seems, can be as childish as the rest of us.
We all have to face the emotional forces that well up from within
   when we fail to get our way.
It is a blow to our esteem at a deeply personal level.
Control has passed from our hands.
No doubt it is even harder for people with power.
They, more often, can force through their will.
But it is a problem for all.
We can moralize about it, Lord, till the cows come home.
But give us that degree of maturity that 'separates the men from
   the boys'.
Give us the wisdom that can bear the refusal of the vineyard.
Give us the strength to be men.

# Up and Away

2 Kings 2.9-15

Up and away in the whirlwind.
It's a hectic ride to heaven.
No smooth road to that unity in the Lord.
The chariots are of fire.

Can I drink the cup of Christ?
Can I stand the baptism with which you were baptized?
There are times when I wish that the chariots would whisk me
    away from the tensions and trials of life.
But the chariots are of fire.
No escape, but a triumph.
You lead a man to you through the midst of the whirlwind.
Lead me to you.

# Linked by Leprosy

2 Kings 5

Three men linked by leprosy;
The soldier whose cure was worth to him 'ten talents of silver, six
    thousand shekels of gold and ten changes of clothing'.
Seven dips in the Jordan are a sign of his faith.
Who wouldn't make offerings to the God of a man of miracles?
The prophet, recognizing himself as no more than the agent of
    God and wishing to accept no payment;
The servant, who is linked to the soldier by more than the curse of
    leprosy.
He too associates well-being and strength and joy with the goods
    that wealth can attain.
Why let Naaman go without accepting what he brought?
Service requires payment.
He plays on a man's sense of indebtedness.
His booty will buy him luxuries, but his dishonesty is stamped on
    him for life.

A man's character is seen in all that he does.
It shines through his actions as a light that guides or as a beacon
    that warns of danger.
The man who has thinks he can buy whatever he wants;
The man who has not covets what the other has;
While Elisha, it seems, remains infuriatingly aloof.

Your concern for a man, Lord, depends on nothing except your
    love. It cannot be bought.
Enable me to respond even when the things I desire are totally un-
    attainable.
Enable me to respond.

# Prophetic Writings

The prophetic writings of Isaiah (with its three collections probably produced by different prophets in different centuries, chapters 1-39, 40-55, and 56-66), Jeremiah and Ezekiel together with the twelve smaller collections of the so-called 'minor' prophets span the period from the eighth to the third centuries BC, presenting a forthright critique of the world of Israel and its neighbours. A detailed survey of these writings is not possible here and we would refer the reader again to the commentaries mentioned in the appendix.

The modern reader will probably feel, and rightly, that some of the writings (Obadiah and Nahum, for example, come to mind) contain much that is of low moral value, which it is extremely difficult to use nowadays with any ease. However, in general, the prophetic faith was of a very profound order, and central to this faith was the belief that the God of Israel was in ultimate control of the historical destiny of his people; and their messages of imminent doom, the day of the Lord, challenged Israel with this fact as much as they gave a prediction of the future. Further, their personal conception of God's dealings with man led them to dwell on the political, moral and spiritual failures of Israel as an act of adultery, an affront to the righteousness and love of God. Their moral outlook was rooted in their faith. Among this collection of biblical books are found insights into the nature of life and the world which rank with the highest in any culture.

# Trampling the Courts

Isaiah 1.10-17; Matthew 5.23-24

'Tramp, tramp, tramp, the boys are marching.'
A song of civil war.
A nation torn apart.
And the choir marches in singing as they come.
'Tramp, tramp, tramp, the boys are marching.'
Tramping can quickly turn into trampling,
And trampling is easy, Lord.
But what lies under our boots?
Trampling is habit,
It is the steady plodding forward along a well-worn path, oblivious
    to all around;
It is the blindness that prevents us seeing anything we do not wish
    to see,
The squashing of your demands under foot.
'Leave your gift at the altar if your brother has anything against
    you.'
My brother?
Who is my brother?
Sharpen our wits, Lord.
Make us sensitive in pursuit of justice, in the cause of the oppressed.

# High and Lifted Up

Isaiah 2.12-18

The 'high places'.
The shrines on the hill.
The lofty cathedrals straining for the stars.
The greatness of a man that has him pushed high on a pedestal.
Why should you wish to pull them down,
To make them low?
Signs of man's achievements are to be admired, not rejected,
For man is your creation.
He is fulfilling something within himself,
Giving form to his aspirations,
Testing himself and his powers to the full.
Isn't this good?
Isn't it creative?
Isn't it right?
And yet his power is your power, Lord,
His strength your strength.
There can be success and glory and fame in arrogating all this to
    himself,
But can there be peace and joy?
Or is the day of pride a day of doom because it leaves man on his
    own?
Our abilities, our powers, our strengths have their foundation in
    you, Lord.
Let us build on this.
Let us seek to mould and shape our world, our future;
But let us see too that our world is your world.
It is you, and not your world, who is the ultimate source of all,
The ultimate goal of our worship,
The beginning and the end.

# How Do the Grapes Fare?

Isaiah 5.1-7,20-29: 10.5-6


History interpreted.
A powerful neighbour casts its shadow over his people.
Assyria in the east threatens their very existence,
The 'rod' raised in readiness to declare God's judgment on their sin.

Lord of history,
Lord of all,
How do you see us, your church, so firmly established in the land?
What do you see growing behind our fences and our walls?
Are the vines running wild, slowly strangling the fruit of the tender
   grape?
Lord of history,
Lord of all,
Tear down our fences and our walls.
Uproot the thorns and briars by whatever means you choose,
Even by means that shock us to the core.
And renew us in service to your world.
Renew us, Lord.
Renew me,
Now.

# Response to Holiness

Isaiah 6.1-8

I am in the basement of the house,
In a small chapel,
Alone.
It is maddening the way my mind wanders from one thing to another as if it were afraid of the silence.
I think, perhaps, I am half-afraid of a silence that might be shattered by a penetrating glimpse of myself;
A silence in which again I am confronted by I know not who or what,
Confronted by the 'Cry' of the universe,
The 'Voice' of holiness,
The Centre of life,
You who are Lord;
A silence in which my world becomes 'charged with the grandeur of God'.

In this moment I am lost and yet found,
Brought low and raised high,
Judged and forgiven.
Here is truth, Lord, and here am I.
Send me out to respond in your world.

# Immanuel

Isaiah 7.1-17

A birth is a time of happiness, of hope,
A time for rejoicing that the new springs out of the old.
Did he point to a pregnant woman of the court, perhaps to the wife
of the king?
Was the birth of her child to be the sign –
The sign that God was with them in spite of their fear of the army
threatening from the north?

The prophet was at it again!
The insufferable bore with his signs!
Why cannot he keep them to himself?
Has not he heard of wishful thinking?
Doesn't he know that even signs of joyous things can blow up in
one's face?
Even 'smouldering stumps of firewood' can cause a conflagration.

I leave Ahaz to his thoughts.
Signs or no signs, Lord, it is good to know that when darkness
looms over the horizon,
When we 'shake like forest trees in the wind',
It is good to know that you are Immanuel.
Be with us by strengthening our faith in you.
Be with us by strengthening our faith in ourselves.
Be with us now.

# Heaven on Earth

Isaiah 11.1-9 (9.2-7; Psalm 2)


Heaven on earth.

The great shortfall between the way things are and the way we yearn for them to be.

An idyllic jungle paradise as a parable of reconciliation.

A blueprint for leadership springing out of the failure of the rulers around them.

Oh for a man who will lead his people into the fulfilment of creation!

Why limit this passage, Lord, to the person of Jesus?

Why not see in it the kernel of responsible authority, the essence of government, the core of relationship?

Let all men share your spirit, Lord.

Let all be part of the messianic vision.

Let 'the earth be filled with the knowledge of the Lord, as the waters cover the sea'.

# An Agent of the Lord

(Second) Isaiah 40.1-11, 21-27: 45.1-13


To be called your anointed when he knew you not;
To be used as your agent in the restoration of the exiles.
What would Cyrus have said about it all?
Would he have been flattered to have had such an exalted sponsor-
ship?
Or would he have been annoyed to find his glory taken away from
him by being used as a pawn in a divine game of chess?
Or, more likely, he wouldn't have cared less about what some
Jewish prophet was saying concerning his role in history.

But here is the point:
'Do you not know, have you not heard,
Were you not told long ago,
Have you not perceived ever since the world began,
That God sits enthroned on the vaulted roof of earth?'
You are the Lord of creation, the Lord of history.
You cannot be contained within the bounds of a nation or a church.
You work throughout your world,
Through the good and the bad, the strong and the weak, the rich
and the poor,
Through those who have no notion of the numinous nor of your
love, as well as through those who have some sense of your
power.
You work through all.
Enable me to glory in this, Lord.
And work also through me.

# 'A Light to the Nations'

(Second) Isaiah 49.1-6

Here's a flash of inspiration, Lord,
A point in the developing understanding of mission.
His people were not to be restored from exile simply to former
    things.
They were to be a 'light to the nations',
To be seen by all as a focus for mankind to be made aware of you.
It was a formidable task,
And a dangerous one,
Because it would expose them to the gaze of the world.
Would men look and give thanks, or look and jeer?

And what about our church now, Lord, your church, us?
Here and there the light does indeed shine in darkness, bringing
    trust and hope in community and the strengthening power of
    your spirit.
Here and there the light glows dimly, flickering like a candle in
    fear of extinction.
And here and there the light seems long since to have burnt itself
    out, leaving behind just a little heap of wax.
Renew, restore, refresh, Lord.
Recall us to your mission from the trivialities that occupy too much
    of your church's time,
    from the things that are 'far too slight a task' for us.
Invigorate with your strength,
For our cause is with you.

# Servants Who Suffer

(Second) Isaiah 52.13-53.12

I have to believe it.

I have to believe that he who carries the sin of a community is your servant, Lord.

The men, the women, the children who choke in the gaschambers of history at the whim of a dictator,

The imprisoned and persecuted,

The trodden down and oppressed,

The wretched and weak,

The scapegoats who suffer for truth in the interests of us all,

I have to believe that in some way their pain, their torture, their suffering, carries redeeming power within it.

The only alternative would be to see suffering as futile and empty and void of all meaning.

And who can bear the harshness of that without life turning sour around him?

This riddle of suffering is part of your hiddenness, Lord.

Strengthen and relieve your servants who suffer for the sake of your world.

# 'New Heavens and a New Earth'

(Third) Isaiah 65.17-19

Who will begrudge him his hope?
His people had suffered plenty in the past,
And now, fresh from exile, had the chance of a new start in a
    restored Jerusalem.
I wish that for them (and for me) the reality would not always fall
    short of the ideal.
Just once, Lord, let us see through the glass clearly.
Just once.
But it's always the same.
I repent, and am forgiven and absolved.
Former things are forgotten by you, Lord, banished to the back of
    your mind.
You create within me a new heaven and a new earth.
You fill me with joy, with delight.
And then, in a flash, the experience is gone, and I am back in the
    old ways.
Thank God your love is infinite.
There is no end to your willingness to create again and again 'new
    heavens and a new earth'.

# The Man and the Nation

Jeremiah 1.4-10, 18.1-11 (Philippians 2.12-13)

The man consecrated by the Lord before he was born, and entrusted
with a mission in spite of his apprehension.

The nation being moulded for destruction like clay in the potter's
hand, yet if it 'turns back from its wicked ways, I shall think
better of the evil I had in mind to bring on it'.

Here is the eternal problem, Lord, of your purposes and our free
will.

The man directed by you, yet with the freedom of responsibility,
the freedom to choose.

The nation shaped in your hands, yet with the freedom to 'turn back
from its ways', to determine its own future.

Who is in control, Lord?

Are you in control?

Are we in control?

How can we both be in control?

I know no answer, except that you work through us.

I feel responsible and able to choose.

The decisions I make, good and bad, are mine.

There is no avoiding responsibility.

But there are times too when I feel that I am responding to something greater than myself.

There are times when, with hindsight, it seems as if I am guided
along a certain path.

I know no answer.

I only know that you delegate your authority.

You gave authority to Jeremiah 'to pull down and uproot, to build
and to plant'.

But unlike the absent landlord you stay around with support.

All I can say, and it is an impossible saying, is that a man 'must
work out his own salvation with fear and trembling, for it is God
who works within him'.

# 'Brace Yourself, Jeremiah'

Jeremiah 1.11-19, 5.1-17, 19.1-15, 27.1-11

'Brace yourself, Jeremiah.'
With this message of yours you will need to be a 'fortified city, a
  pillar of iron, a wall of bronze'.
You preached treason – bow to the yoke of Babylon.
You preached doom – the people are to be shattered into pieces like
  some cheap earthenware jar.
You preached justice and righteousness against those with their
  faces set 'harder than flint',
  against the 'lusty stallions neighing after a neighbour's wife'.
With a message like this you will need all the help you can get.

The uncongenial word is the hardest word to speak.
It's as hard on him who speaks as on him who hears,
For the more sensitive he is the more it entangles him in a web of
  embarrassment.

The uncongenial word is the hardest word to hear.
It incurs an odium in direct proportion to its truth.
Who worries much about the lie that openly proclaims itself as
  such?
The man we want to remove is the one who cuts near to the bone,
  or at least mixes sufficient truth with the untruth.

'Brace yourself, Jeremiah.'
I am only half on your side.

# 'All is Well'

Jeremiah 6.9-15

Reassurance.

Sometimes it is needed.

When it is the truth, it can give strength to one who knows no
strength.

But massive reassurance when the need is for a challenging truth
leads only to the crash.

It is a temptation, Lord, to say the easy word.

'Peace, peace....'

'All is well....'

It is temptation to say the word that all want to hear,

The word that reinforces the way we all live,

The word that uplifts while leaving us precisely where we have
always been,

The word that no one could take amiss,

The word that never gets to grips with reality.

'... but there is no peace!'

'... nothing is well!'

The problem of reassurance is the problem of truth.

Reveal the truth, Lord.

Strengthen me to reveal it,

The truth that challenges as well as the truth that reassures.

# Rejected

Jeremiah 9.2-3, 15.10-21, 20.7-18

He felt totally rejected.
'All men abuse me.'
'For me they care nothing.'
Why was it that men turned their backs on the teaching he believed
    came from you?
Was he being deceived, deluded?
Were you a 'brook not to be trusted, whose waters fail'?
Would that he could escape into a solitude far from the pressures
    of life.

It is a common enough feeling, Lord,
When a man's offer of help is thrown back in his face,
When he speaks the truth that his hearers are eager to label a lie,
When his reading of a situation is rejected out of hand and often
    from ignorance,
When his exploration of new paths discomforts others who feel
    themselves threatened and attack in return.
It is a common enough feeling, Lord, that either fans the incipient
    flames of suspicion within, or turns us back on ourselves in a
    fit of self-questioning doubt.
Give a sense of proportion, Lord,
And give encouragement.

# The Leopard's Spots

Jeremiah 13.23


It is not true that the colour of a man's skin makes no difference.
It does.
It makes as much difference as the meaning for a man of the face
of the woman he loves.
It makes as much difference as the place in which a man has his
roots and in which his character was formed.
It makes as much difference as all the differences between one man
and the next.
And this can be glorious and creative, Lord, that people are different
and unique in the sight of you and of each other.
It can be glorious and creative that all the differences in the world
are encompassed by your love.
But when the coin turns, the glorious thing sinks to the insidious
evil of isolation, the raising of barriers against all who are seen
to be different, who might pose a threat,
And ultimately to total isolation if all are indeed different from all.

'Can the Nubian change his skin,
Or the leopard its spots?
And you? Can you do good,
You who are schooled in evil?'
Can you, you who turn the glorious thing into an insidious evil?
I pray that you can.
I pray that Jeremiah is being too fatalistic.
Or is it I who am naive?

Let the analogy be broken.
Be a Lord of change.

# When the Heat is On

Jeremiah 17.5-8

There is a last minute crisis,
A hitch in the plans.
The telephone rings and goes on ringing.
Advice is being proferred from all sides,
Conflicting advice about what should be done, how we should act.
And the last state of confusion is worse than the first.
Whose advice should be taken?
Whom should I trust?
I am 'among the rocks in the wilderness, in a salt land where no
  man can live'.

I need some peace, Lord, some quiet,
A moment to think,
To reflect.
'Blessed is the man who trusts in the Lord ...
He shall be like a tree planted by the waterside ...
When the heat comes it has nothing to fear ...
And does not cease to bear fruit.'

'Lord, in you have I trusted;
Let me not be confounded.'

# Figs

Jeremiah 24.1-10

Prophetic licence.
Either black or white.
Some figs are good, some figs are bad.
Is it a safe analogy for people, Lord? –
However great his sympathy for the exiles and their suffering;
However great his anger towards the survivors in Judah:
People are more complex than figs.
Let me be cautious of sweeping judgments.

# A New Covenant

Jeremiah 31.27-34, 32.1-15

Locked in prison for preaching the fall of Jerusalem,
He still gambles seventeen shekels of silver on a future for the
    nation.
He read the signs of the times as the end of an era, the breakdown
    of the covenant,
But the Lord is faithful to his nature and will someday re-establish
    himself in the hearts of his people.

Our relationship, Lord, is the constant breaking and re-establishing
    of covenant.
It is I who break it,
And you who re-establish it.
It happens so often it would seem so light a thing.
It happens so often I come almost to accept its inevitability.
Yet I think that even this is perhaps better than a state of constant
    anxiety that one day you may weary of setting me up again.
Lord, I repent; I am not worthy.
Renew our bond once again.

# Ezekiel the Strange

Ezekiel 1.1-3.15


He was shaken by his experience, Lord.
For seven days he stayed dumbfounded.
Did he wonder what was happening to him?
Visions,
Hallucinations,
Was he going mad?
His experience touched the depths of his personality.
He was filled to the brim with your word, and 'it tasted as sweet as
    honey'.
His inner experience, odd though it was, authenticated itself.

Ezekiel is the type of the strange man, the very strange,
Yet the man who still perhaps has some profound insight about life,
    an insight that is easily missed, obscured by his strangeness.

You can work, Lord, through all men.
You can use whatever personality a man has, however odd it might
    seem to those around him.
Let us not be put off by the bizarre.
Enable us to cope with the unusual.
Enable us to try to get inside it to see what it says.

# Responsibility

Ezekiel 3.16-21


A man is an individual, responsible for his actions.

But he is also a member of a community and responsible for others.

The problem is to decide the limits between these two responsibilities, Lord.

When does concern to change another turn into interference with his freedom?

There was a child who ran into the road, to be pulled back by a passer-by.

A life had been saved.

There was a preacher trying to restrict the activities of his congregation, burning with zeal to prevent their corruption by the 'wicked and evil ways' of something many would feel to be right.

Was the fruit of the sermon a latent friction or guilt?

Was life being lessened?

The watchman needs to watch himself.

Give guidance, Lord.

Let all that I am, all that I do communicate a responsible concern.

Be the watchman within me.

# Depressing Signs

Ezekiel 4.1-5.17

The tell-tale tile with its message of siege.
The rationed food and divided hair.
That uncomfortable rest on one side after the other.
Striking signs, Lord,
Prophetic actions,
Done, no doubt, to great effect, to burn into the consciousness of the people.
I have a built-in bias against seeing you in such inhuman terms as an agent of destruction.
And here is the prophet proclaiming your wrath.
His interpretation of the events that were befalling his people is natural enough – to think that apostasy and moral laxity ought to be punished.
But is it right?
Or is it a rationalization of events in terms of his faith?
There is always the danger, Lord, that we see you as a bigger and better model of ourselves, whose displays of wrath can be justified because of your holiness.
And yet your power is the love that allows us to destroy you on a cross.
In the midst of depressing events in history, Lord,
Bring us to our senses,
Use us, your people, to restore, renew, re-create.

# False Prophecy, or True?

Ezekiel 13.1-16

I wish it were as easy as this, Lord,
To know the source of inspiration.
Sometimes it is when prophecy leads only to hate – or to love.
I wish it were always easy to tell whether beliefs and attitudes and
    feelings were the expressions of your indwelling spirit,
Or only internal prejudices, conditioned by forces foreign to your
    nature.
Usually it is a mixture of both.
You can only speak through a man as he is, and he is a mixture of
    sin and grace.
But who speaks your truth and how much of your truth when there
    are conflicting views of your will?
You leave us to decide for ourselves, Lord.
Draw me closer to you.
Inform my mind.
Bring me into union with you.
And purge that part of me which produces a message that is as false
    to humanity as it is to you.

# He Stands Alone

Ezekiel 14.12-20

He is an alcoholic,
In and out of prison,
In and out of jobs,
Abandoned by his wife.
He stands alone.
Not even Noah, and Daniel and Job could save him.
They could do a lot.
They could support him as he tries to fight off the bottle, and be
    there at a moment of crisis.
They could be around to listen to the stream of guilt and depression
    whenever he falls.
But at the final count he stands alone,
Accountable for himself.
It is no help to him or anyone else to apportion blame,
To say that he is his own worst enemy, that it is all his own fault.
Or to blame it all on to the circumstances of his life.
He knows the score.
He knows that he stands alone.
To take this away from him would be to remove the one remaining
    piece of his personal responsibility and identity.
I see no future for him, Lord.
But you give me the faith to continue to be there against impossible
    odds.

# A Cemetery Comes to Life

Ezekiel 37

A vision of dramatic reversal.
A cemetery comes to life.
Bones are reborn in the plain of death.

It was a large ward, almost square, with easy chairs around the
  walls and dining tables in the middle and a few flowers here and
  there.
On the chairs the old ladies sat, mostly doing nothing, some now
  totally out of touch with reality, with no future but death.
How would it be possible to stay or work in this environment
  without an assurance of the ultimate meaningfulness of all life?

You give hope, Lord, in hopeless situations.
Give hope.
You declare victory for life in the very midst of death.
Declare the victory and make it known.

# The Whore of Hosea

Hosea 1.2-3, 3.1, 6.10-7.16, 11.1-11, 14

His wife was unfaithful, yet he loved her.
He loved her as you, Lord, love the man who has no time for you.
The power of judgment is withheld.
The power that withers and destroys all in its path,
The power that annihilates hope in a man and turns all that it
    touches to dust,
The power that leaves no room for forgiveness and love.
This power you will not unloose,
Because you are 'God and not a man, the Holy One in our midst'.
You are as close to a man as a groom to his bride.
And in this closeness are all the seeds of healing,
All that can bring out the best in a person and lead him to whole-
    ness.
All that helps to fulfil our humanity.
Come close, Lord.
Stay close,
Especially when it seems as though you are as far away as can be.

# The Outpouring of the Spirit

Joel 2.28-32; Acts 2.14-21; Galatians 5.22

'The day shall come when I will pour out my spirit on all mankind.'
Do we look for the spirit, Lord, in the babblings of Pentecost or the
    quality of life to which Paul alludes?
Or do we look to both?
'The great and terrible day of the Lord' was the day of failure,
When total gloom surrounded their lives,
When their future plans were back in the melting-pot,
When any attempt to put a face on it, with a touch of bravado,
    would have been at the best only partly convincing.
They were shattered.
You were dead.
It was only later that this 'great and terrible day' became the day
    of triumph,
The day of 'love and joy and peace',
The day on which they could not contain themselves,
The day when they had to share their new vision of life.
Your spirit, Lord, is poured out on all who at any time or in any
    place experience those positive gifts that are its fruit.
You do not wait for us, thank God, to 'invoke you by name'.

# 'The Day of the Lord is Darkness'

Amos 2.6-16; 5.16-24

The terrible indictment.
'The day of the Lord is darkness, not light.'
You are present, Lord, in the poor whose heads are ground into the
    earth,
In the destitute sold for a pair of shoes.
You are present in the girl profaned by father and son,
In the prophets stifled by those who fear the truth.
In so far as it is done to them, it is done to the Lord.
You are present, Lord, but you are not seen.
'The day of the Lord is indeed darkness, not light.'
Your presence in people is a hidden presence.
We can be singing our hymns,
We can be delighting in our worship,
Only to find that you have long since left,
And are now to be found where life is at its darkest.
'The day of the Lord is darkness.'
Lord, 'Let justice roll on like a river.'
Let it be seen,
Let us reveal it,
Where darkness is so dark that it cannot be missed.

# Oh to be Back among the Sycamore Trees!

Amos 7.12-15

Did he wish he were back at home with his sycamore trees,
Far away from the pressures of prophecy?
I would not hold it against him, Lord.
There are times when responsibilities weigh heavy,
Times when I long for the easy life,
Where decisions no longer need to be made,
Where worries and anxieties about myself, about others, about
    situations no longer disturb my peace,
Where all restlessness can be banished for ever.
There are times when the demands seem too demanding.
'I am no prophet ... I am a herdsman and a dresser of sycamore
    trees ... but the Lord took me and said to me, "Go ...".'
Strengthen me, Lord, in the way you would have me go.

# Revenge

Obadiah

There are strong feelings here seething below the surface,
Feelings that long to be unleashed against his enemies.
For him the time has come for the tables to be turned.
The fortunes of his people have been far from favourable,
But 'soon the day of the Lord will come on all the nations',
And they will be treated as they have treated others.
He is certainly honest about his emotions, Lord.
No pangs of conscience,
No feelings of guilt instilled over the years by a straightlaced
    morality!
The desire for revenge is a very human emotion.
We sometimes try to give it an exalted value by attributing it to
    you.
If you are a god who can revenge himself in hell on those who ignore
    you, then can we not do the same?
To love my neighbour is at least a possibility,
But to love those who stir within me strong feelings of aggres-
    sion ...?
How am I to cope with these feelings, Lord?
I cannot pretend that they do not exist.
Keep me alert to their presence lest I clothe them with justifications.
'And dominion shall belong to the Lord',
Even at the depths of my soul.

# The Whale is No Escape

Jonah 1-2

He wanted to escape, Lord.
He wanted to evade the demands of life.
He wanted to avoid what had to be.
He could not face a city notorious for all that he despised.
He welcomed the waves.
He wished for peace, he thought, at any price.
But the price was too high.
The womb-like security of the whale turned claustrophobic.
His peace became a prison.
He was unable to run away from his responsibilities because that
    was to run away from himself.
Lord, you send us to Nineveh.
Much of the time we take ship to seek that whale.
Strengthen our wills.
The whale is no escape.

# Sin Pays a Wage

Jonah 3-4; Romans 6.22-23

Poor Jonah.
Not only was there no escape, neither did he have the satisfaction
of seeing your judgment on sin.
It is not always easy to accept your forgiveness of others, Lord,
because then I too must forgive.
There are times when I find myself sitting under a tree, apart from
it all, waiting for you to act.
'For sin pays a wage, and the wage is death', and those men's sin
is great.
But instead of judgment, forgiveness.
Am I to go on judging?
Can I forgive?
Can I?

# Walk Wisely Before your God

Micah 6.1-8

What comment can there be, Lord, on a passage that pierces to the
heart?
'What shall I bring when I approach the Lord?
How shall I stoop before God on high?'
I know all about the calves and the rams and the ten thousand
rivers of oil.
I know all about the external things we use to buy you off.
More and more services,
More and more worship.
Drum up the troops to sing of our sin.

'I brought you up from Egypt,
I ransomed you from the land of slavery.'
You give men freedom, Lord,
Freedom from the frown of fortunes beyond our control,
Freedom to be ourselves.
Yet the more I see of my responsibility to be myself, the more I
seem to fail.
The gulf for ever widens between what is and what ought to be.
I clamber up a step to see the stairs disappearing yet further into
the distant height.
You have a case against me, Lord.
Stay your hand.
Join with me.
Let us walk together.

# And God Said: Let there be Darkness, and there was Darkness

Nahum

I suppose that there were mitigating circumstances, Lord,
Circumstances to excuse his exultation,
At the rape of Nineveh,
The assault on Assyria.
His people had suffered greatly at the hands of this arrogant and
    cruel neighbour.
And now the boot was on the other foot.
At last 'the battering ram is mounted against their bastions'.
And they can sin no more.

But how am I expected to use such a prophecy now?
Am I to clap my hands in joy at the destruction, even if it is
    deserved?
Strong words,
Strong emotions,
A verbal barrage of hate.
'The Lord is a jealous god, a god of vengeance,
The Lord takes vengeance and is quick to anger.'
God made in the image of man.
And god said: let there be darkness, and there was darkness.
And god saw everything that he had done, and behold it was very
    bad.
It is no good, Lord.
This book is closed.
I cannot for the life of me see its worth.

# An Answer

Habakkuk 1.1-2

Is anyone at home?
Am I talking to myself?
Is it all self-deception?
'How long, O Lord, have I cried to you, unanswered?'

Has the answer, then, got something to do with my responsibility?
Is that it?
You give me optimism and hope to live in your world,
To begin on adulthood,
To live as a man,
And only occasionally the strengthening sense of your presence.
Let this be sufficient, Lord.

# Comfort in Confrontation

Habakkuk 1.5-13; 3.17-19

You work through mankind, Lord.
Yours is the power, he says, behind their chastisement at the hands
    of Babylon.
You work through people who know you not,
Who are as guilty – or even more guilty than the rest of us.

Does that man's sarcasm hold some message for me?
Is his anger a word from the Lord?
Are you somewhere within him challenging me to faith?
You are present in the most unexpected places, unexpected people,
Confronting me with myself.
I sense judgment, sometimes when face to face with the most un-
    likely person,
The person with whom I feel that I have least in common.
Is it perhaps your judgment, Lord?
That sarcastic drunk, for whom I had little time, cut me down to
    size.
At the times
When judgment strikes,
When all seems lost,
When the signs are against me,
When the finger is pointed towards me,
When forces stronger than myself bear down in judgment upon
    me,
Comfort me in the confrontation.
Give strength.
Give courage,
So that even then, and especially then, I might 'rejoice in the God
    of my deliverance'.

# Dies Irae

Zephaniah 1.2-2.3

Cosmic collapse.
What a waste!
'I will sweep the world clean of all that is on it.'
The end of a creation that held such promise.
The prophet puts an admission of failure on your lips, Lord.
He despaired of the world.

For some there are times when it might as well come to an end,
Days now – no need to wait for that end – 'of anguish and affliction,
Of destruction and devastation,
Of murk and gloom'.
That man over there, in the depths of depression –
It seems, he says, as if you have gone berserk and 'dropped him in
    the muck'.
But he goes on living.
There is a glimmer of hope.
'It may be that you will find shelter in the day of the Lord's anger.'
Life still seems better than death.

Give life, Lord,
To him,
To me,
To all.

# Zerubbabel for Messiah?

Haggai 2.1-9, 20-23; Zechariah 4.6-9; 6.9-13; 1 Corinthians 3.16-17

Back from exile,
With Zerubbabel for king,
'The Branch'[1] from the stump of David's tree,
The Messiah in their midst.
They must rebuild the temple.
Haste was imperative.
At any moment the Lord might establish his messianic kingdom in
  Zion,
Vindicating his people,
And bringing to an end oppression from foreign neighbours.

Free-floating ideas eventually come to rest around objects and
  people.
The pathetic little community returning from the east retains its
  faith in grandeur.
It hopes for great things from Zerubbabel and temple, the focus of
  its aspirations.
They were deluding themselves, Lord,
As some say that I delude myself by claiming even greater things
  for the man from Nazareth.
But then you stand the test of time.
There are two thousand years of witnesses
That 'here is a man named the Branch',
Who 'shoots up from the ground ... and builds the temple of the
  Lord'.
And that temple we are.

[1] Assuming at Zechariah 6.11 that Joshua the high priest is inserted in
error for Zerubbabel.

# A Dead End

Malachi

There is no surprise over their disenchantment, Lord.
He was trying his best with the old, old story.
'If you placate God, he may show you mercy;
If you do this, will he withhold his favour from you?'
That direct link between good works and reward, bad works and
  punishment.
What future is there here? —
For the man who sees the evil prospering?
'What do we gain from the Lord of Hosts by observing his rules
  and behaving with deference?
We ourselves call the arrogant happy;
It is the evil-doers who are successful.'
What future is there here for the man who tries hard to pull himself
  up by his bootstraps only to become more conscious of failure?
  — if he can avoid the pit of self-righteousness.
It is a dead end.
There is no future here.
But you have overturned the system, Lord.
Quality of life and action is not the bait with which we try to hook
  your love —
It is rather the fruit of a man's awareness that he has a place in
  the world.
It is the fruit of a man's awareness that your love is the source of all.
Bring us to see where we stand with you.
Work your righteousness within us.

# Wisdom

The wisdom literature of Israel includes the Old Testament books of Proverbs, Job and Ecclesiastes. Proverbs is probably a post-exilic collection of sayings spanning many centuries and dealing with the down-to-earth matters of human life. Job and Ecclesiastes also probably belong to the post-exilic period, the former being a profound exploration of the problem of human suffering while the latter presents a rather weary view of life. The 'human situation' is the focus of these books and it is to them that we now turn.

# The Fear of the Lord

Proverbs 1.7, 4.7 (1 Corinthians 1.24)


She really was afraid, Lord,
Afraid of the consequences of her actions,
The cosmic consequences of your all-powerful wrath.
Fear filled her conscience and her conscience filled her mind.
She was armed with text upon text that supported and increased
    her fear.
You were the tyrant, Lord, angered by her sin,
The angry parent unable to accept her unacceptable parts.
'The fear of the Lord is the beginning of wisdom.'
But her fear of you, Lord, was the end of her peace of mind.
Fear is reverence and fear is dread.
Will the one replace the other in her experience?
Can an inhibiting dread give way to a healthy reverence?

You are the wisdom of God, the beginning of all, the source of
    life.
To live in you is to live in wisdom.
To live in you is to gain understanding.
To live in you is the heart of life 'though it cost you all you have'.
And it will be costly for her, Lord, to exorcise the tyrant to make
    room for you.
Be with her,
Be with me,
As the foundation of our future.

# Go to the Ant

Proverbs 6.6-11


I don't think that he has stayed in any job for more than a week or
    two.
He leaves or is sacked whenever he doesn't get his own way.
He is still a child for all his twenty-one years.
But he does not yet know poverty.
His unemployment benefit provides.
The really sad thing about it, Lord, is not this danger of material
    poverty.
It's the growing sense within him that society owes him a living,
    that we should all drop everything and rally round to provide
    full-time satisfaction for his whims.
How he can play on our emotions, Lord!
The way he lives is becoming a way of life, which makes him
    virtually unlivable with.
How long can he live off the capital of an unfortunate childhood
    without it lessening his chances of growth?
How long should he be encouraged to degrade himself by sponging
    continually on the sympathy of others?
The ant, perhaps, is too computerized a creature to use as an
    example.
But a communal effort, a compulsion to serve, an achievement of
    some value – might he not be happier with this?
Some of us urge him to work and leave him rejected.
Others feel so sorry for him that it inhibits any note of challenge.
How, Lord, to communicate understanding and love coupled with
    an encouragement to turn outwards from himself?

# An Enticing Woman

Proverbs 7.6-23, 9.1-6


Why should the devil have all the best tunes?
So he portrays Wisdom as an enticing woman, as enticing as the
  prostitute scented for the kill.
Heady wine, this Wisdom.

Lord of Wisdom, Lord of all,
In Jesus you summoned men to follow.
You call, you entice, you attract,
You force a decision.
Our response, our 'yes' or our 'no', is a decision, a committal.
Lord, in you do I trust; strengthen my trust.

# Talking and Listening

Proverbs 10.19, 17.28; James 1.19; John 1.14

There are three of them, Lord, and how they can talk!
The woman is eager to make contact and seeks to help, but her
   continual talk only serves to frighten people away. She seems
   to be threatening them with a constant bombardment of words.
The man is out to impress with his knowledge and insight, but
   instead of the reassurance he craves he finds himself resented by
   those who prefer not to have their ignorance revealed even to
   themselves.
The girl protects a deep insecurity by a superficial camouflage of
   speech. She hopes to hide herself, to kid others into believing
   that all is well. But the more she chatters, the more anxiety she
   reveals.

Talking and listening – the problem goes deeper than a proverb.
It is a problem of identity, security, worth.
The one who listens communicates an acceptance, or a judgment,
   to the one who speaks.
He communicates that the speaker is either worth listening to or
   not worth talking to.
To hold one's tongue can be as traumatic as to talk too much.

You, Lord, are the Word of God.
You speak and remain silent.
You comfort and confront.
You strengthen and challenge.
Let us listen and let us speak, but let us be slow to speak.

# Peace and a Sword

Proverbs 15.1; Matthew 10.34, 23.13-15, 27-33

What a session, Lord!
With feelings that are normally hidden deep within bursting to
    the surface for all they were worth.
We were going at each other hammer and tongs.
I have even forgotten how it started.
But it soon became apparent that both of us felt the need to force
    our views down the other's throat.
A ceaseless attack and counterattack of 'sharp words' kept our
    tempers at boiling point.
Did we feel threatened, Lord?
Did our anger spring from anxiety?
A reasoned calm, a 'soft answer', is perhaps the only answer.
But it is not always like this.
I remember the words of passion, of fire, the sharp words spoken
    with feeling against complacency and hypocrisy and pride –
'Alas for you ... I come not to bring peace, but a sword' –
The words that kindled the tempers of those who fixed you to a
    cross.

Let me seek peace and let me pierce with a sword.
But for God's sake
Let me get the timing right.

# A Capable Wife

Proverbs 31.10-31

An ode to creature comforts!
Oh, for a wife such as this!
Slippers warming by the fire, meals on the dot, perfection at every
turn – domestic bliss!

I wonder what the wife feels, Lord.
Is it all joy and satisfaction, do you think?
Or is there some guilt, as she feels that her talents might be slipping
away from her in the hectic round of family routine?
Is there some resentment at being so exclusively tied to the home?

Here and everywhere, Lord,
Be the source of freedom within the frustrations and restrictions of
life.

# Life is Toil

Ecclesiastes 1.1-3.12; Romans 8.18-28

He is old in experience.
Life is toil.
One thing after another.
The joy is gone.
Knowledge and wisdom, wealth and pleasure, all is empty, devoid
of real meaning.
Sometimes it is like this, Lord, like 'chasing the wind', like an
endless treadmill,
A grinding routine, fixed as firmly as if it were written in the stars,
with all things, all events, the whole future waiting for us
silently, meaninglessly, in the wings.
There are times when nothing satisfies,
When high hopes of fulfilment peter out into nought,
When 'there is nothing new under the sun'.
It is like this now, Lord, for many a man.
The Speaker speaks for them.
'The whole created universe groans in all its parts as if in the
pangs of childbirth.'

Make sense, Lord, of our inarticulate groans.
Give point to life.
Add a dimension to our experience.
Lift us out of the rut.
Give us your perspective.
Bring us to comprehend your work from beginning to end,
To see again the growing 'divinization of our activities and our
passivities', the transforming of all that we are, the onward evolu-
tion of your world to its final culmination.
Bring us to you.

# Out of the Whirlwind

Job

Why, Lord, why, Lord, why?
Do you rebuke a man for asking the question?
Do you rebuke a man for seeking why he should suffer so?
Out of the whirlwind you spoke to Job of your power.
Why, then, is suffering built into the very fabric of life?

He sits in a wheelchair now.
It seems an eternity since those times he played tennis only a few
    years ago.
That was before he knew that he was to spend the rest of his life
    with useless legs.
He hides his hostility for much of the time, except from himself.
Let him vent his wrath, Lord.
Let those around him be strong enough to take it and withdraw
    its sting.

But why, Lord, why, Lord, why?
What are you saying to a man through suffering?
What are you saying through your suffering on the Cross?
Speak, Lord, out of the whirlwind.
Speak, and give me the courage to confess:
'The Lord gave and the Lord has taken away; blessed be the name
    of the Lord.'

# The Unveiling of the Future

These four meditations are based on stories from the book of Daniel written in the middle of the second century BC at the time when Antiochus Epiphanes was ruler of Syria and overlord of Judah. Antiochus sought to ban all traditional Jewish practices and placed an altar to Zeus – 'the abomination of desolation' – in the Temple in Jerusalem. The Apocryphal books of the Maccabees tell of the revolt for independence which broke out in 167 BC, and it was probably at this period that the book of Daniel appeared. The first six chapters of Daniel contain patriotic stories of past heroes set within the Exile in Babylon with an account of their legendary witness to the Jewish faith under similar persecution. The second half of the book is apocalyptic writing reviewing past history as if it were still to happen for the purpose of revealing that the whole course of history and the destiny of nations were in the control of God. These chapters present a picture of bizarre symbolism and 'reveal' that catastrophic disasters will overcome the wicked world as God breaks into history at the beginning of his reign. The anonymous author assumes the name of Daniel and writes as if he were living several centuries earlier. The book and its cryptic unveiling of the future would encourage those Jews who were remaining loyal to their faith in the face of persecution and martyrdom. This book, perhaps more than any other in the Old Testament, requires to be understood against its background before it can make any sense at all.

# The Fiery Furnace

Daniel 3

You are the Lord of fire.
Present in a fiery furnace.
Present in the heat of life.
Present in situations of horror and despair.
Present in the prisons that incarcerate men for their beliefs.
Shadrach, Meshach and Abednego were lucky ones, Lord. They
    came out unscathed.
Not all are as lucky.
Not all withstand the tyrannies of life and remain unharmed.
You are with men in their suffering, in their aloneness and ignominy
    and death.
Be with them.
Be with them through us who are your limbs.
Give even a glimmer of hope in hopeless situations;
For where there is no hope, there is nothing.

# The Writing on the Wall
Daniel 5

A purple robe, a chain of gold and third place in the kingdom, all
    this he was offering – only to be told that his reign was found
    wanting.
Perhaps he would have been happier not to have known.
To learn an unpleasant truth is unpleasant indeed.
To have it publicly proclaimed is even worse.
The writing was on the wall.
There is death in the desecration of sacred things.
And all things are sacred, Lord, set apart as your creation.
To destroy and misuse is to annihilate all that turns existence
    into life.
Waste, pollution, the unloved child.
The sacred desecrated.
The holy profaned.
The whole of creation is yours, Lord.
A universe consecrated by your love.
The writing is on the wall.
Write it large and bold,
Indelibly in our hearts.

# The Lions Fail Again

Daniel 6

An encouragement to faith when faith is needed most.
A call to confidence and courage.
A summons to suffering.
And the lions fail again.
I remember the story of Proctor, Lord.[1]
The ordinary man, the man in the street.
Sometimes in church, often not.
Not a man of much doctrine.
A man caught up in the seventeenth-century savagery of Salem's
  hunt for witches and the devil's men.
Embroiled in a mass hysteria, a communal myth.
All he had to do was to denounce a witch or two and admit his
  secret allegiance with the devil.
But he saw the fanaticism to be false.
He refused to say what he knew in his heart to be wrong.
This ordinary man who knew himself to be no better than anyone
  else, no paragon of virtue, struggled through to integrity, to
  honesty.
So he was labelled as the devil's man.
His threat to the common myth ensured his execution and his great-
  ness.
The lions got their meal, but not the man.
Courage is a nebulous quality, Lord, giving an extra dimension to a
  man.
Its presence or its absence is only seen as the lions approach, as the
  door of the den is sealed.
This measure of strength is the measure of your indwelling spirit.
You radiate strength from the cross.
Share your resources, Lord.
Share them with all who are persecuted for holding to their integrity.
Share them also with me.
Let the lions always fail.

[1] Arthur Miller, *The Crucible*.

# The Reality of Evil and the Glory of Man

Daniel 7

Man, made in the image of God,
Remakes himself as a beast.
But the beasts will not prevail.
Man is to be called again to become the company of 'the saints of
    the Most High'.
Life is in this vision, Lord, life in a nutshell.
The reality of evil and the glory of man.
The oppression, the anger, the pride of beasts and the ultimate
    power, the sovereignty, the triumph of man.

You define both, Lord.
You define the glory and triumph as you stagger under a cross.
You define evil and pride as that which puts you there.
You are the one 'coming like a man with the clouds of heaven',
The cosmic Christ, the universal man, the fulfilment of humanity.
'Behold the man!'

# Appendix 1: A Brief Bibliography

*Commentaries*

William Neil, *One Volume Bible Commentary*, Hodder & Stoughton 1962. Compact, readable and good value for money.

A. S. Peake, *Commentary on the Bible*, ed. Black & Rowley, Nelson 1962. A much larger work for reference.

The series of *Torch Bible Commentaries* and *Layman's Bible Commentaries* on individual books, published by SCM Press.

*General Books*

John Bowden, *What About the Old Testament?*, SCM Press 1970. A short introduction to modern studies on the Old Testament.

Mark Gibbard, *Why Pray?*, SCM Press 1970. See especially chapter 6 for a discussion of the use of the Bible in prayer.

Norman Gottwald, *A Light to the Nations*, Harper & Row 1959. A fairly detailed, illustrated work introducing the writings of the Old Testament and the history of Israel.

E. W. Heaton, *The Old Testament Prophets*, Penguin 1961.

John Otwell, *A New Approach to the Old Testament*, SCM Press 1967. A readable introduction to the way in which scholarship helps our understanding of the Old Testament.

Rolf Rendtorff, *Men of the Old Testament*, SCM Press 1968. A way into the history of Israel through the men who made it.

P. S. Robinson, *A Layman's Guide to the Old Testament*, SPCK 1957. A short, straightforward study of the background of the Old Testament.

# Appendix 2: Some Dates and Facts

## SOME DATES

Mid second millennium BC  The Patriarchs

| | |
|---|---|
| Thirteenth to eleventh centuries BC | The Exodus from Egypt<br>Conquest of and settlement in Canaan<br>The Judges |
| End of eleventh century BC | Monarchy established under Saul, David and Solomon |
| 922 BC | Kingdom divided into Israel in the north and Judah in the south |

---

The Kingdom of Israel 922-721 BC     The Kingdom of Judah 922-587 BC

Israel fell to the Assyrians, who were themselves conquered by the Babylonians (Nineveh, the Assyrian capital, fell in 612 BC). The Babylonians conquered Judah with the fall of Jerusalem in 587 BC

---

Sixth century (587-538 BC)   The Exile in Babylon

The Exile ended when the Persians under Cyrus took Babylon. Cyrus decreed the restoration of the Jewish community in 538 BC

---

| | |
|---|---|
| End of sixth century to mid second century BC | The Jewish community re-established and came under the influence successively of the Ptolemies and Seleucids. |
| 167 BC | The Maccabaean Revolt broke out against the Seleucid ruler Antiochus Epiphanes. |

# FACTS

## Three 'Major' Prophets

The prophetic ministry of Isaiah (chapters 1-39, excluding 24-27 which belong to the later period of apocalyptic writings) was in Jerusalem in the second half of the eighth century. His experience of the holiness of God led him to denounce the sin of his people, and although he preached a day of doom he still held out hope that God would be with a remnant of his people. The Messianic passages (9.2-7, 11.1-9) possibly belong to a later period.

Second-Isaiah (chapters 40-55) is the work of an unknown prophet living with the exiled Jews in Babylon about the middle of the sixth century. He believed that the God of creation and history would use the unbelieving Cyrus to re-establish the exiled Jews who were to be 'a light to the nations'.

Third-Isaiah (chapters 56-66) forms a collection of oracles from the post-exilic period in Palestine, a time in which the legalistic framework of life was hardening

Jeremiah belongs to the period immediately preceding the exile (626-586 BC). He too denounces the sin of his people, but despairs of the leopard changing his spots, and was rejected by his contemporaries. He retains, however, a belief that God will make a new covenant with his people.

Ezekiel's prophecy was delivered in the sixth century and reflects the life of an exile in Babylon (though some of the collection may have been delivered in Jerusalem before the city fell in 587 BC). His behaviour is often distinctly odd and 'ecstatic' and this tends to put him out of favour with the modern reader.

## Twelve 'Minor' Prophets

The pre-exilic prophets:

Amos and Hosea exercised their ministry in the middle of the eighth century BC in the years before the northern kingdom of Israel was destroyed in 721 BC by the Assyrians. Amos proclaimed that the coming 'Day of the Lord' would be a day of darkness and judgment on the people for their transgressions, though he also held out a small ray of hope that a remnant might be spared. For Hosea the intimate relationship between God and his people had been broken by the latter's unfaithfulness and apostasy, and marriage symbolism is used to develop this point.

Micah was a contemporary of Isaiah and prophesied during the last quarter of the eighth century BC in the southern kingdom of Judah. He prophesied disaster on Israel and Judah and denounced social injustice. It may be that only the first three chapters of the book belong to the man named Micah, but this does not of course mean that the remaining chapters are any the less important because their authorship may be anonymous.

Nahum focussed on the collapse of Nineveh, the capital of Assyria, in 612 BC.

Zephaniah and Habakkuk may also belong to the end of the seventh century BC. The former book contains a passage on which the Latin hymn, Dies Irae, is based, and the latter raises the question of why the Chaldaeans, 'that savage and impetuous nation', should be the instrument of God's chastisement of his people.

The post-exilic prophets:

Haggai and Zechariah (though chapters 9-14 form a separate collection possibly dated as late as the third century BC) are associated with the rebuilding of the temple in Jerusalem in 520 BC at the end of the exile in Babylon.

Obadiah, Malachi and Joel are of uncertain date somewhere between the sixth century and the fourth. The author of Obadiah roundly denounced Edom, the book of Malachi mirrors religious decline and that of Joel came out of an occasion of a severe plague of locusts which was seen as a possible harbinger of the Day of the Lord.

The book of Jonah, which also belongs in this period, is clearly different from the other Canonical prophetic books in being a religious romance. It points to the implications of a man's relationship with God.

# Index of Passages

*The Early Days*

| Genesis | 1.26-3.24 | Adam is Everyman | 3 |
|---|---|---|---|
| | 4.1-16 | Cain is a Marked Man | 4 |
| | 6.5-8.19 | The Chaotic Flood | 5 |
| | 9.18-19 | Sons of Noah | 6 |
| | 11.1-9 | Babel | 7 |
| | 12.1.4 | Abraham's Faith and Mine | 8 |
| | 22.1-14 | Abraham's Faith and Mine | 8 |
| | 28.10-22 | Dreams | 9 |
| | 32.24-30 | It is a Struggle to Pray | 10 |
| | 37.5-28 | How Joseph Travelled from Canaan to Egypt | 11 |
| | 39.21 | Fourteen Cows, Seven Fat, Seven Thin | 12 |
| | 41.1-45 | Fourteen Cows, Seven Fat, Seven Thin | 12 |
| | 45.4-5 | Fourteen Cows, Seven Fat, Seven Thin | 12 |
| Exodus | 3 | The Day Moses Saw the Bush | 13 |
| | 4.10-16 | The Day Moses Saw the Bush | 13 |
| | 14.5-31 | A Rough Sea Crossing | 14 |
| | 25.10-22 | An Ark for Salvation? | 15 |
| | 32.1-6 | Aaron's Uncertainty | 16 |

*The Tablets of Stone*

| Exodus | 20.1-3 | Divinity All Round | 19 |
|---|---|---|---|
| | 20.4-6 | Idols Modern Style | 20 |
| | 20.7 | A Name in Vain | 21 |
| | 20.8-11 | The Problem of Sabbath | 22 |
| | 20.12 | Parents | 23 |
| | 20.13 | Killing | 24 |
| | 20.14 | Man and Woman | 25 |
| | 20.15 | Property is Sacred, They Say | 26 |
| | 20.16 | Witness the Truth | 27 |
| | 20.17 | The Ox and the Ass | 28 |

*Joshua and the Judges*

| Joshua | 2.1-21 | The Harlot's Scarlet Cord | 31 |
|---|---|---|---|
| | 6.1-27 | And the Walls Came Tumbling Down | 32 |

| | | | |
|---|---|---|---|
| Judges | 7.1-25 | Gideon's Gallant Three Hundred | 33 |
| | 8.22-23 | Gideon's Gallant Three Hundred | 33 |
| | 13.2-16.31 | Samson | 34 |
| Ruth | | Black, White, Brown, Yellow | 35 |

## Four Kings, Four Prophets

| | | | |
|---|---|---|---|
| 1 Samuel | 1.1-2.11 | Hannah's Hope | 39 |
| | 3 | The Listening Servant | 40 |
| | 8.4-22 | Who is King? | 41 |
| | 10.17-25 | Who is King? | 41 |
| | 17 | David's Goliath | 42 |
| | 18.28-20.1 | Saul's Vendetta | 43 |
| | 28.3-19 | The Witch of Endor | 44 |
| | 31.1-7 | The Witch of Endor | 44 |
| 2 Samuel | 1.17-27 | The Magnanimity of David | 45 |
| | 5.1-6.15 | A City of Hope and Despair | 46 |
| | 12.1-15 | 'You Are the Man' | 47 |
| 1 Kings | 3.3-28 | That Proverbial Wisdom of Solomon | 48 |
| | 5 | The House that Solomon Built | 49 |
| | 7.51-8.13 | The House that Solomon Built | 49 |
| | 10.1-13 | Wealth, Wealth, Glorious Wealth | 50 |
| | 17 | More Miracles | 51 |
| | 18.17-40 | Contest on Carmel | 52 |
| | 19.1-18 | What is Hidden in the Earthquake? | 53 |
| | 21 | The Vineyard that Caused the Sulk | 54 |
| 2 Kings | 2.9-15 | Up and Away | 55 |
| | 5 | Linked by Leprosy | 56 |

## Prophetic Writings

| | | | |
|---|---|---|---|
| Isaiah | 1.10-17 | Trampling the Courts | 59 |
| | 2.12-18 | High and Lifted Up | 60 |
| | 5.1-7, 20-29 | How Do the Grapes Fare? | 61 |
| | 6.1-8 | Response to Holiness | 62 |
| | 7.1-17 | Immanuel | 63 |
| | 10.5-6 | How Do the Grapes Fare? | 61 |
| | 11.1-9 | Heaven on Earth | 64 |
| | 40.1-11, 21-27 | An Agent of the Lord | 65 |
| | 45.1-13 | An Agent of the Lord | 65 |
| | 49.1-6 | 'A Light to the Nations' | 66 |

| | 52.13-53.12 | Servants Who Suffer | 67 |
| | 65.17-19 | 'New Heavens and a New Earth' | 68 |
| Jeremiah | 1.4-10 | The Man and the Nation | 69 |
| | 1.11-19 | 'Brace Yourself, Jeremiah' | 70 |
| | 5.1-17 | 'Brace Yourself, Jeremiah' | 70 |
| | 6.9-15 | 'All is Well' | 71 |
| | 9.2-3 | Rejected | 72 |
| | 13.23 | The Leopard's Spots | 73 |
| | 15.10-11 | Rejected | 72 |
| | 17.5-8 | When the Heat is On | 74 |
| | 18.1-11 | The Man and the Nation | 69 |
| | 19.1-15 | 'Brace Yourself, Jeremiah' | 70 |
| | 20.7-18 | Rejected | 72 |
| | 24.1-10 | Figs | 75 |
| | 27.1.11 | 'Brace Yourself Jeremiah' | 70 |
| | 31.27-34 | A New Covenant | 76 |
| | 32.1-15 | A New Covenant | 76 |
| Ezekiel | 1.1-3.15 | Ezekiel the Strange | 77 |
| | 3.16-21 | Responsibility | 78 |
| | 4.1-5.17 | Depressing Signs | 79 |
| | 13.1-16 | False Prophecy, or True? | 80 |
| | 14.12-20 | He Stand Alone | 81 |
| | 37 | A Cemetery Comes to Life | 82 |
| Hosea | 1.2-3 | The Whore of Hosea | 83 |
| | 3.1 | The Whore of Hosea | 83 |
| | 6.10-7.16 | The Whore of Hosea | 83 |
| | 11.1-11 | The Whore of Hosea | 83 |
| | 14 | The Whore of Hosea | 83 |
| Joel | 2.28-32 | The Outpouring of the Spirit | 84 |
| Amos | 2.6-16 | 'The Day of the Lord is Darkness' | 85 |
| | 5.16-24 | 'The Day of the Lord is Darkness' | 85 |
| | 7.12-15 | Oh to the Back among the Sycamore Trees! | 86 |
| Obadiah | | Revenge | 87 |
| Jonah | 1-2 | The Whale is No Escape | 88 |
| | 3-4 | Sin Pays a Wage | 89 |
| Micah | 6.1-8 | Walk Wisely Before your God | 90 |
| Nahum | | And God Said: Let there be Darkness, and there was Darkness | 91 |
| Habakkuk | 1.1-2 | An Answer | 92 |
| | 1.5-13 | Comfort in Confrontation | 93 |
| | 3.17-19 | Comfort in Confrontation | 93 |
| Zephaniah | 1.2-2.3 | Dies Irae | 94 |

| Haggai | 2.1-9, 20-23 | Zerubbabel for Messiah? | 95 |
| Zechariah | 4.6-9 | Zerubbabel for Messiah? | 95 |
| | 6.9-13 | Zerubbabel for Messiah? | 95 |
| Malachi | | A Dead End | 96 |

*Wisdom*

| Proverbs | 1.7 | The Fear of the Lord | 99 |
| | 4.7 | The Fear of the Lord | 99 |
| | 6.6-11 | Go to the Ant | 100 |
| | 7.6-23 | An Enticing Woman | 101 |
| | 9.1-6 | An Enticing Woman | 101 |
| | 10.19 | Talking and Listening | 102 |
| | 15.1 | Peace and a Sword | 103 |
| | 17.28 | Talking and Listening | 102 |
| | 31.10-31 | A Capable Wife | 104 |
| Ecclesiastes | 1.1-3.12 | Life is Toil | 105 |
| Job | | Out of the Whirlwind | 106 |

*The Unveiling of the Future*

| Daniel | 3 | The Fiery Furnace | 109 |
| | 5 | The Writing on the Wall | 110 |
| | 6 | The Lions Fail Again | 111 |
| | 7 | The Reality of Evil and the Glory of Man | 112 |

*New Testament Passages*

| Matthew | 5.23-24 | Trampling the Courts | 59 |
| | 10.34 | Peace and a Sword | 103 |
| | 23.13-15, 27-33 | Peace and a Sword | 103 |
| John | 1.14 | Talking and Listening | 102 |
| Acts | 2.14-21 | The Outpouring of the Spirit | 84 |
| | 2.42-45 | Property is Sacred, They Say | 26 |
| Romans | 6.22-23 | Sin Pays a Wage | 89 |
| | 8.18-28 | Life is Toil | 105 |
| 1 Corinthians | 1.24 | The Fear of the Lord | 99 |
| | 3.16-17 | Zerubbabel for Messiah? | 95 |
| Galatians | 5.22 | The Outpouring of the Spirit | 84 |
| Philippians | 2.12-13 | The Man and the Nation | 69 |
| James | 1.19 | Talking and Listening | 102 |
| 1 Peter | 2.9 | Who is King? | 41 |